COMMON SCENTS STRATEGIES

Tricks of the Trade for Attracting Deer

OUTDOORSMAN'S EDGE®
GUIDES

COMMON SCENTS STRATEGIES

Tricks of the Trade for Attracting Deer

RICHARD COMBS

CREATIVE
OUTDOORS™

DEDICATION

This one's for Sylvia.

Trade paperback edition first published in 2006 by

CRE**A**TIVE
OUTDOORS™

An imprint of Creative Homeowner®, Upper Saddle River, N.J.
Creative Homeowner® is a registered trademark of Federal Marketing Corp.

Front cover image: Don Jones. Back cover image: Richard Combs. All inside images by author unless noted otherwise.

Published by: Woods N' Water, Inc.
Peter and Kate Fiduccia
P.O. Box 550
Florida, NY 10921

Printed in the United States of America
10 9 8 7 6 5 4 3 2 1
Library of Congress Control Number: 2006929873
ISBN: 1-58011-307-9

CREATIVE HOMEOWNER®
24 Park Way
Upper Saddle River, NJ 07458

TABLE OF CONTENTS

INTRODUCTION

More years ago than I care to remember, I sat atop a ladder stand by a pond on a farm in central Kentucky. I faced the pond, and to my right was a wooded hillside sloping down into a small drainage. Straight ahead, a logging road wound its way toward me and skirted the pond. To my left the hillside was mostly open pasture land, but a thicket came up to the road, just beyond the pond, creating a bottleneck of sorts—a spot where deer crossed the road to avoid the open pasture. It was the late muzzleloader season, cold, and the air was tinted pink in the fading light from the sunset behind me.

When I heard thrashing sounds in the brush off to my right, I knew exactly what it was. A buck was staging in the thicket about 60 yards off, waiting for darkness before crossing the road or entering the pasture. For a good ten minutes he worked on those saplings, and then the woods went silent. I tensed a little in anticipation, then caught a glimpse of him straight ahead beyond the pond, about 80 yards out. In the thick cover, I could see a respectable eight-point rack, but little else. The buck started my way, but stopped in high grass. I peered through my scope, anxious to get off a shot before the light faded completely, but the cover was too thick. When the buck turned and disappeared into the

The author with a dandy 10-point Iowa whitetail.

woods, I sat up, disappointed. My hunt that day was over. I stood in preparation to climb down when I heard a stick pop and spotted movement. He was back!

I dropped to my seat and put my eye to the scope again, resting the Markesbery muzzleloader over the cushioned railing, not knowing for sure if the light would be sufficient. It was. The buck stopped about 70 yards out in the clear, quartering toward me slightly. I put the crosshairs tight behind the right shoulder, squeezed off a shot that cracked sharply in the cold air, then sat back and tried to relax, confident I'd soon be following a short blood trail to my trophy. I picked my lit cigarette up from the fork of the tree beside me and inhaled deeply, leaned back with satisfaction and blew a few smoke rings, then crushed the butt against the tree limb and prepared to climb down from the stand.

The cigarette is the point, of course. I'm happy to report that I quit smoking not long after that incident, but in those days I smoked regularly while on stand. Chances are, if you've hunted a few years, you've heard similar stories from deer hunters who put their lit cigarettes in the fork of a tree as a buck approached, shot the buck, then picked the cigarette up to finish the smoke

The point of such anecdotes is seldom left to speculation, and is usually explained along the lines of, "If they're downwind of you they're gonna smell you no matter what you do, and if they're not downwind of you, they won't smell you no matter what you do."

Some variations on the theme might include, "and who's to say a deer knows what cigarette smoke is, anyway? The Indians used to sit in campfire smoke to use it as a cover scent."

To most any deer hunter, those are interesting issues. Is it true that it's impossible to beat the nose of a deer? That if the wind is right they won't scent a hunter, and if it's not they will, no matter what precautions the hunter might take?

And what about cover scents? Do they work? Can a creature that can detect onion at a concentration of one onion molecule per *billion* other molecules fail to detect human odor because it's mixed with a few drops of fox urine?

And what about food scents? Can concentrated or artificial acorn scent fool a deer? Will a deer respond to the scent of apples if there are no apple trees in a given area? Will it respond to apple scent if the deer in question is a deep-woods deer that has never encountered an apple?

How about curiosity scents? Do they work? Will a deer alter its route to approach the source of an aroma that is totally unfamiliar to it?

Do pheromones and other sexual scents fool deer?

Do any of these aromas frighten or repel deer? Can a scent that attracts a deer on one day cause it to be alarmed on another day?

The tendency of hunters to focus on the whitetail's prodigious olfactory capabilities makes perfect sense, given that their sense of smell is their number one defense. Deer are far from blind, though, and more than one hunter has muffed an opportunity not because a deer caught his scent, but because it saw him.

We can examine the make-up of the whitetail's eyes to provide evidence about how they see, but this is only one piece of the puzzle, and doesn't tell us how they interpret or react to what they see. Most hunters are aware that deer do not see colors as humans do, but do deer see any color at all?

What about their depth perception?

Do they have the visual clarity that humans have for seeing small details?

Similarly, we suspect that the hearing of deer is superior to that of humans. Is it, though, or are deer as prey species simply more alert to the sounds around them?

Do deer hear the same frequencies as humans or are they, like dogs, capable of hearing high-pitched sounds that are beyond the range of the human ear?

Wild turkeys are said to be able to fix the precise location of distant sounds–an amazing feat for a creature with no external ears. Do whitetails have a similar ability?

There are several difficulties in answering these and similar questions pertaining to the sensory capabilities of deer. The first has to do with the impossibility of getting inside an animal's head. The best we can do is observe its behavior and interpret it. The tendency is to attribute human characteristics to animals–what biologists refer to as anthropomorphism.

A perfect example of this comes to mind: when I was a youngster we accepted it without question when our elders explained to us that a wise old buck would send does or younger bucks down the trail ahead of it, to alert it to danger from hunters. That was their interpretation of the situation when they noted that a buck often came down the trail shortly after a doe came by. From a human perspective, it makes perfect sense. The question is, do deer think in such terms, and would a buck actually be able to get a doe to precede it down a trail to protect the buck from danger? These days hunters are far more inclined to think that the bucks are simply following the does. We can't get inside the head of a given buck to prove the more modern theory, but sufficient evidence exists in its favor to convince most of us that it is correct.

Another difficulty is the essentially subjective nature of a sensory experience such as smell. Scientists have wrestled for years with the problem, struggling

Years ago, hunters believed that the buck would send a doe out ahead of him. Today, most of us think a buck simply follows the doe(s).
CREDIT TED ROSE.

to produce for industry an "electric nose." In fact there are several such devices now available. Useful as they may be for specific purposes, none of them come remotely close to the capabilities or the sensitivity of the human nose–which is itself far inferior to that of most other mammals. Knowing exactly what an animal is or is not capable of smelling, how and why it reacts to given smells, how many smells it can distinguish between at one time, which smells it responds to instinctively, and how long it takes to associate a given smell with danger–these are all complex and difficult questions.

Then there are all the variables. Temperature, humidity, wind direction and velocity, all play a role in scent. When we note that a deer appeared to react to a given scent at 60° F, 70 percent relative humidity, five mph winds, can we assume the deer would react at 25° F, 30 percent relative humidity, with 25 mph winds? If you doubt those variables could have an effect on scenting ability, talk to anyone who regularly hunts with bird dogs or hounds. They will quickly assure you that the ability of their dogs to scent a covey of quail or track a rabbit can vary greatly with temperature, humidity, and wind.

Finally, much of what we know (or think we know) about the subject tends to be based on anecdotal evidence. Consider the following scenario: A man is wearing a carbon suit and sees a big buck circling behind him, downwind. He's convinced the buck will bust him any moment, but instead it stops broadside directly downwind, pausing long enough for the hunter to get off a successful shot. Chances are no amount of evidence to the contrary is going to convince that hunter that wearing the carbon suit did not contribute to his success. In fact, he'll probably swear by it.

On the other hand, if another hunter in a similar situation is busted, he's likely to conclude that the carbon suit is worthless, and no amount of evidence to the contrary will convince him that carbon suits can be effective in suppressing odor.

In a similar vein, a hunter wearing full head-to-toe camo, who is confident he is motionless, will probably give credit to the camo if a deer walks by and doesn't see him. If one deer spots him, though, nothing is likely to convince that hunter that wearing camo makes a difference.

The fact is, of course, that none of these scenarios proves anything. There are simply too many variables involved to come to a reasonable conclusion on the basis of one or two incidents, especially without having a great deal more information at our disposal.

Before I convince you (and maybe myself) that answering any of the questions we've considered above is hopeless, let me remind you how much knowledge we have gained about the management, hunting, and behavior of white-tailed deer in the space of one generation of deer hunters.

I recall vividly a day when I was one of a car full of high school students and the driver hit the brakes to stop for a doe crossing the road. We sat staring in silent wonder–we had never seen a deer in Ohio before. Now in parts of Ohio, as in so many similar areas, deer numbers are out of control.

My father traveled out of state for a week-long hunting trip each fall, and when I was seventeen I was deemed mature enough to join him and his buddies

A whitetail's nose is its number one defense–and that is easy to see when you know that it can detect onion at a concentration of one onion molecule per billion other molecules! CREDIT TED ROSE.

in deer camp. The strategy was simple: we scouted for tracks, droppings, or beds. Rubs and scrapes were curiosities. The accepted explanation for rubs was that deer made them when scraping the velvet from their antlers. Scrapes were–well, we didn't know what scrapes were–beyond knowing they were made by bucks. Any concentration of sign of any kind was deemed a good spot to hunt.

What we knew about the natural history of white-tailed deer–their habits and behaviors–we could have put in a thimble with room left over. And a good portion of what was in that thimble was just plain wrong. (I've already mentioned the widely held theory that bucks sent does ahead of them down the trail as hunter bait.)

We did not hunt from trees, and would have thought the notion funny. Though we were aware that deer probably did not see color as humans do, and that the plaids we wore tended to break up our outlines, it did not occur to us to wear camo clothing. We knew that bucks grunted, but did not attempt to call or rattle deer. We had some vague ideas about the rut, but I don't recall connecting rubbing or scraping with it. In fact, it was only years later I realized that most of the variations in our success from one year to the next had to do with whether or not we were hunting before, during, or after rutting activity. And though we knew enough to try and stay downwind from where we expected to see deer, we knew nothing of thermals and thought little about the ways the landscape can affect wind currents. Nor would it have occurred to us to pass up our chosen spot because the wind was blowing the wrong way.

Today, the experienced deer hunter can bore a biology professor to tears with his knowledge of white-tailed deer behavior, talking endlessly about everything from which kind of acorns deer prefer; to when they prefer alfalfa over soybeans and vice versa; how they use any of a number of different glands to communicate with other deer; the significance of the various grunts, bleats, shorts, and wheezes deer are known to make; what triggers the rut; when and where bucks are most likely to respond to rattling; the significance of a rub line; the difference between a small scrape at the edge of a field and a large scrape in a staging area; when bucks shed their racks; how does signal their readiness to breed; and on and on.

Granted, in some cases we're only theorizing–but the theories are usually based on knowledge and on countless hours of experience and observation.

We've already learned a few things about the role of scent in deer hunting. We may not know precisely how and why deer use scrapes and rubs, for instance, but we know that they deposit glandular secretions, saliva, and urine in ways that other deer recognize and respond to. And in contrast to the days when an army of red-wool-plaid hunters spread out through the woods to lean against trees all day, with a vague awareness that it was preferable to be downwind of any path deer might choose to travel, today's hunters have a far more sophisticated understanding of the role played by thermals, as well as how the landscape shapes air currents to form backdrafts, swirling air currents, and eddies in ways that confound all but the most careful hunters.

The answers, I'm convinced, are out there. As with other aspects of animal behavior, ultimate proof may not always be a realistic goal. What *is* a realistic goal is increased knowledge and understanding, theories that better explain observed behavior, and hunting strategies that are more effective. The answers come from scientific and technological breakthroughs, from scientific study, from countless hours of observation, and sometimes, from just plain thinking through the question and arriving at logical conclusions. As with any inquiry, the answers often lead to additional questions. Each step along the way represents progress. I harbor no notions of writing the definitive book on the role of scent and other sensory perceptions in deer hunting. What I do believe we have done with this book–and I say we not out of modesty, but because so many have contributed to the knowledge contained in the pages that follow–what I do believe we have done with this book is provide an in-depth, comprehensive look at the complex role of scent and other sensory capabilities in deer hunting, in a way that will contribute to knowledge and effective hunting strategies.

Richard Combs
Cincinnati, Ohio 2006

THE SENSE OF SMELL:
HOW IT WORKS

A hunter doesn't need to know how the sense of smell works to know that it is preferable to stay downwind of his quarry, or to know that the scent wick he is hanging from a tree is unlikely to have an effect on a deer bedding in a thicket upwind from the wick.

Beyond those basics, though, many hunting strategies in which scent is an issue (and that would be most of them) come down to matters of judgment. Understanding how scent works is one piece of the puzzle that can help a hunter decide when the use of a certain product is a waste of time and money; or when it is likely to be effective; whether to hunt a given stand in the morning or in the evening (and when, in terms of scent, it doesn't matter); when to hunt close to a bedding area and when to stay farther from it. The hunter whose time is limited can even use such knowledge to decide when to take off work and head for the woods, and when to wait for a higher percentage opportunity.

Smell is arguably the most direct and most precise sense. Vision is a matter of perceiving light reflected from an object, hearing a matter of detecting sound waves created by a moving object. Touch is a crude sense at best, while taste can distinguish only sweet, bitter, sour, and salty. (Taste is 80 to 90 percent smell.)

A hunter spots a movement in the shadows, but what is it? He often doesn't know, and excited hunters are notorious for seeing deer or other game animals that aren't there-sometimes with tragic results. A hunter hears leaves rattling, but what is causing it? He might make a good guess, but often it's impossible

A deer's nose, as compared to a human nose, has a larger area inside that detects smell and a larger portion of their brain is dedicated to detecting odors as well. CREDIT TED ROSE.

to tell. Taste and touch require direct contact, and seldom play a role in hunting.

Contrast those senses with smell. Biologists have suggested that humans can distinguish up to 10,000 different aromas, but more recent theories suggest that the number is almost infinite. No two substances smell exactly alike. One researcher has compared various substances to products with bar codes; each substance has its own bar code, and the human nose/brain can detect the difference between any of them.

Furthermore, smells are almost never forgotten. Poets have long suggested that smell is the most evocative or nostalgic sense, insisting that a rare smell from years past can bring back vivid memories from childhood or even infancy. Psychologists agree, citing lab experiments with humans and animals confirming that of all the senses smell seems most closely linked to memory, and that once encountered a given odor is seldom forgotten.

Granted, some smells–particularly those rarely encountered and perceived as not being strong smells–can leave humans uncertain about their origin. On the other hand, though we occasionally may not know what we smell, we rarely smell something that isn't there, or misidentify a smell we know. Any adult who is sure he smells an orange that turns out to be an apple, or is confident he smells a banana that turns out to be spoiled milk, is probably suffering from some sort of neurological disorder.

In fact, so sophisticated is the human nose that science and industry are unable to duplicate it, or even come close to matching it. There are at least a couple of "electronic noses" on the market, but their applications are very limited. Industries such as the perfume industry, the deodorant industry, the wine industry, and others, still rely on panels of human judges to analyze the aromas of their products. Experienced medical technicians can often tell by the aroma from a petri dish or a urine sample exactly which illness a given patient is suffering from. Microscopes or chemical analyses simply confirm what they already know. And any lab technician who smells high concentrations of toxic or explosive gasses will clear the room without stopping to consult his instruments.

We stated earlier that scent is arguably the most direct sense. What that means is this: when you detect an odor, you are coming in direct contact with molecules from the source of the odor. Whether it is the smell of hot asphalt after a summer shower, an orange being peeled, or a lady's perfume, molecules are being released into the air which make their way into the nostrils and adhere, or are "captured" by molecules on a moist patch far inside the nasal cavity. Receptors send a message to the brain, which interprets the aroma. That is an extremely simplified explanation of the process, but it is essentially what happens.

Not every substance has an aroma, because not every substance is volatile enough to release molecules into the air in sufficient quantities to be detected. Steel, for instance, does not really have an aroma, nor do certain synthetic materials such as some plastics. Heat, humidity, and air pressure can affect both the rate at which molecules are released, and the ability of the nose to detect them. Boiling, for instance, can transform a slight aroma into a strong one. On the other end of the spectrum, low pressure on airplanes greatly reduces odors–which is one reason airplane food has little flavor.

The portion of the brain that interprets smells is a very primitive part of the brain, which may be in part why it so easily triggers vivid memories. It is also closely linked to instinctive behaviors. Some researchers have determined, for instance, that human infants no more than a few days old will react adversely

Under ideal conditions, it has been noted that whitetails will react to odors up to a half-mile away. CREDIT TED ROSE.

to certain unpleasant smells, and positively to other, apparently more pleasant, smells. There is also evidence that infants can distinguish their mother's unique smells, and even that mothers can distinguish their own infants by their smells. Women, for unknown reasons, seem to have a sense of smell superior to that of men. Smell is also related in unknown ways to emotional well-being. People with anosmia–a total inability to smell as a result of brain injuries or other trauma–are often emotionally depressed. And ridicule it as we might, there is evidence that aroma-therapy actually works. Moods can be elevated by the smell of certain substances such as lavender.

We can surmise that most of what is true about scent for humans is true

Knowing that your scent will more than likely be driven to the ground during a snow storm, take advantage of this and dress warmly and head afield. CREDIT FIDUCCIA ENTERPRISES.

for deer as well–that is, that it is associated with a primitive part of the brain that involves instinct, that once encountered smells are rarely forgotten, that certain smells are pleasant while others are unpleasant.

One thing we do know is that the sense of smell of the deer is far superior to that of humans. Various researchers have made claims ranging from six times better all the way up to 10,000 times better, but placing a precise number on the difference is unimportant. What is important is the realization that deer smell things we don't, and at much greater distances. The nose of a deer is much larger than that of a human, and the mucous patch inside the nose that detects smell is considerably larger, as is the portion of the brain that is involved in interpreting odor. Under optimum conditions, white-tailed deer have been observed to react to odors from as far away as half-a-mile.

What are optimum conditions for a white-tailed deer to detect odors? Most researchers agree that deer smell best when humidity ranges from 20 to 80 percent, with temperatures between roughly 40 and 90 degrees Farenheit, with winds under 15 miles per hour.

Extremely humid conditions, including rain, heavy snow, and even dense fog, tend to reduce dispersal of scent, often driving it to the ground. Very dry conditions tend to dry out the nasal passages, preventing scent molecules from adhering to the mucous membranes in the nose.

Extreme temperatures can also dry out the nasal passages, as well as affecting the volatility of scent-producing substances.

Wind is a trickier issue. Little or no wind means that scent is not dispersed, while high winds dry out nasal passages and, presumably, scatter scent molecules widely, often swirling them around in ways that make it difficult to determine the strength or the location of an odor.

Then there is the issue of thermals. As temperatures rise, air currents tend to rise, carrying scents with them. Conversely, falling temperatures tend to create downdrafts. In the absence of wind, such downdrafts can carry a hunter's scent to the ground, where it spreads away in all directions. ■

SCENT AS
COMMUNICATION

Deer are social creatures. While a doe without fawns might occasionally be seen alone, and while bucks often go their separate ways, especially during the rut, it is far more common to see deer in groups. Does usually travel in family groups, with one or two of their offspring, and sometimes the offspring of the offspring for a family group of several generations. Bucks spend much of the time winter through summer in bachelor groups, sometimes large ones. Winter, in particular, often sees deer forming into larger bands.

While deer are not strictly speaking territorial, they do have their home ranges, which vary in size depending upon season and quality of habitat. Does may occupy an area as small as 60 acres under ideal conditions, though ranges of several hundred to a thousand acres are more common, and bucks may range over areas two-to-five times this size. Both bucks and does form pecking orders, with dominant and sub-dominant bucks and does inhabiting a given area. Home ranges of both bucks and does tend to overlap, and both bucks and does will tolerate familiar deer in their areas far more readily than they will tolerate strangers.

Smell plays an important role in the social life of deer. They use it to keep tabs on which deer are in their area and when. Scents also tell them something about the dominance, the health, and the breeding status (in heat or in rut), of the deer living in or passing through their area.

Like most ungulates (hoofed animals), deer pay particular attention to

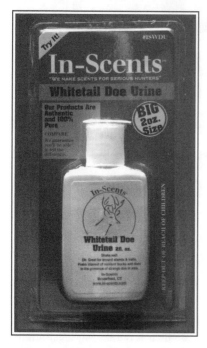

Using doe urine scents, like this one from In-Scents, is an excellent way to help lure a deer into your location. CREDIT IN-SCENTS.

urine. (There will be a lot more about this in subsequent chapters.) They rarely pass up fresh urine without checking it out. Deer urine, fox urine, cow urine, or even human urine–it really doesn't matter, deer seem curious about it and will often stop to scent check it when they encounter it.

Deer also leave scent from various glands on various parts of their bodies. Not all glands are related to scent, and there is even some disagreement about whether or not various organs are or are not glands. Beyond that, there is some disagreement about the precise function and the relative importance of various glands. Having said all that, biologists share some widely held theories regarding the different glands that seem to be related to scent and communications, based on observations of behavior and simple deductive reasoning.

THE TARSAL GLAND

Probably the gland with which most hunters are most familiar is the tarsal gland. Tarsal glands are located on the inside of the hocks of the hind legs of both bucks and does. Both sexes squat and urinate on these glands during the rut, rubbing their hind legs together. Normally a buff or whitish color, the tarsals turn dark brown or black during this time. This process helps deer locate one another during the rut.

This shot of a tarsal gland was taken during the spring when it is not darkened from urine during the rut. CREDIT FIDUCCIA ENTERPRISES.

Presumably, some combination of secretions from the tarsals, with the urine, offers deer some indication of one another's sexual readiness, and possibly degree of dominance and general health.

THE METATARSAL

Metatarsals appear as small, whitish tufts of hair on the outside of the lower hind legs of bucks and does. Since they have no ducts, they are technically not glands, nor do they produce any known substance. Their purpose is not fully understood, but some observers speculate that they release odors to signal fear or aggression. One of the more interesting theories related to the metatarsals is that, when deer are bedded and the metatarsals

The metatarsals are outside the lower hind legs of bucks and does. Their function and purpose has been discussed and researched many times over the years. CREDIT FIDUCCIA ENTERPRISES.

are in contact with the ground, they can sense minute vibrations, alerting deer to the approach of anything walking.

The forehead gland is between the eyes and the base of the deer's antlers. When a buck makes a rub, he deposits scent from this gland that is unique to him. CREDIT TED ROSE.

THE FOREHEAD GLAND

The forehead gland is, as you might suspect, located on a buck's forehead between the eyes and the bases of the antlers. When a buck rubs his antlers on trees or shrubs, he leaves secretions from these glands behind as a sort of calling card, announcing his presence to other deer in the area.

THE PREORBITAL GLANDS

Not far from the forehead glands are the preorbital glands, which are located just in front of the eye socket. Their location might suggest they are tear ducts, but they don't produce tears, although they do produce secretions that lubricate and cleanse the eyes. They also produce a waxy substance which, along with the forehead gland secretions, appears to be left behind on trees, branches and shrubs during rubbing activity, or when bucks are thrashing their antlers in thickets. This substance has a smell similar to that of ammonia, and is strong enough to be easily detected by humans.

The preorbital glands are located just in front of the eye sockets. They also leave a secretion when the buck makes a rub or rubs his eyes against an overhanging branch of a scrape. CREDIT TED ROSE.

THE INTERDIGITAL GLANDS

Deer also possess interdigital glands in the cleft between the front hooves. These emit odors that are left in their tracks, allowing other deer to trail them. Based on observations of the ways bucks react to the trails of does in heat, many biologists believe that the interdigital glands, as well as urine and tarsal glands, offer some indication of the breeding status of does. At the same time, when deer stomp their hooves at unfamiliar, unknown, or threatening objects in the woods, the interdigital gland secretions are released in larger quantities to remain on the ground. Many biologists speculate that this scent can alert other deer to danger in the area for hours afterward.

THE JACOB'S GLAND

Finally, the Jacob's gland is located on the roof of the mouth. As with many ungulates, it is used by the buck in detecting estrous females. In a behavior called "flehmen," the buck extends his head and neck and curls back his upper lip for several seconds, which apparently intensifies olfactory stimuli and

One of the more fascinating field observations of bucks is when you see a buck like this one who is flehmening. He is detecting pheromones from an estrus doe's urine. CREDIT TED ROSE.

allows him to detect pheromones present in the urine of does prior to and during peak estrous.

As you can see, the relationships and functions of all these various glands and behaviors are complex and not fully understood. Biologists have collected some curious bits of information that may be clues to putting the whole puzzle together, but which remain mysteries for now. For instance, fawns often urinate over their hind legs and rub them together when they are frightened, whereas older deer, both bucks and does, tend to engage in this behavior to display aggression or dominance. While tarsal glands, interdigital glands, and rub-urination seem to serve the same general function of sexual cues and indicators, the function of the metatarsals is less clear. It was once speculated that they released scents warning other deer of danger, but more recent thinking suggests that deer rely primarily on visual and auditory cues such as snorting, stomping the ground, or raising the tail as warning signals.

RUBBING AND SCRAPING

We've made some indirect references to rubbing and scraping activity, but these are worth a closer look, since they are unique to deer and important to hunters in understanding the activity patterns of deer in a given place and period of time, and in developing hunting strategies, including the use of various scent products.

Though there is some disagreement about the purposes and the significance of rubbing and scraping, biologists (and hunters) have learned a great deal about these behaviors in the last two decades or so.

Rubbing activity begins in the later summer, when bucks begin to lose the velvet from their antlers. In fact, most hunters once believed that rubbing was nothing more than the means by which bucks got rid of the velvet. That may be one function of rubbing, but of course it does not explain why bucks continue to rub, and even to rub more frequently and vigorously, long after the velvet is

Note the bark and lichens on this buck's brow tines. Bucks deposit scent from their forehead and possibly pre-orbital glands when rubbing trees.

Rubs serve as visual as well as olfactory cues. The size of this tree, as well as the depth of the gouges, indicates a sizeable buck made the rub.

gone from the antlers. Most experts today accept the theory that rubs are a visual, olfactory, and auditory calling card, indicating the presence of bucks. The forehead, and possibly the preoribital glands, leave scent on the rubs revealing the identity of the deer that made the rub, or that contributed to it, since in some cases numerous bucks use the same rub. It is also possible that these scents, as with urine and tarsal gland secretions, offer some indication of health and relative dominance in the herd. Visual evidence alone–and we'll revisit this subject in a subsequent chapter–can offer hunters some information about the size of the buck that made the rub, but whether other bucks and does understand the visual information (beyond an awareness that a buck made it) is something we can only speculate about. The noise made by a buck as it rubs a tree or thrashes about in saplings certainly conveys its presence to any deer within hearing range, and may be an expression of dominance as well.

Scraping activity is a fascinating instinctive behavior. Though deer occasionally

This buck is in the process of making a scrape. He is licking and chewing the overhanging branches above the spot where he will paw it free from leaves and grass. CREDIT TED ROSE.

make what appear to be haphazard, casual scrapes, other scrapes involve a complex routine. Every such scrape is characterized by a licking branch or branches overhead. These are small limbs, usually four to six feet above the ground. Typically, a buck approaches a suitable area and begins nuzzling, licking, and sometimes chewing on, the end of the licking branch. In some cases the buck

Since does frequent scrapes made by bucks, one tactic is to put out doe estrus urine in a scrape to make the buck think a doe has recently visited "his" scrape. CREDIT FIDUCCIA ENTERPRISES.

will stand on its hind legs to reach higher limbs. All this activity deposits saliva and glandular secretions on the licking branch. Then the buck paws up the ground beneath the licking branch to clear away leaves and scratch down to bare soil. The final step is to squat somewhat, with the hind legs together, and urinate over the tarsal glands and into the scrape, often rubbing the hind legs and tarsal glands together.

We'll look at scrapes in more detail later in the book, but it's worth mentioning here that most scrapes are one-time only scrapes, and will never be revisited, while a select few will be revisited by the same buck, and in the case of some strategically located scrapes, may be visited repeatedly by numerous bucks in an area.

Does occasionally create scrapes, too, and will sometimes visit and contribute to, the scrapes made by bucks. Their urine, and possibly the secretions from other glands as well, will indicate to bucks how close the does are to being in heat. Bucks often scent check their scrapes, sometimes simply passing by downwind of them, in search of hot does.

PHEROMONES

Deer hunters have been hearing a lot about "pheromones" in recent years. Strictly speaking, pheromones are any chemical substance released by an individual to influence the behavior of, or produce a desired response by, another individual of the same species. Insects in particular are noted for their use of pheromones. Social insects such as bees and ants use them for relatively complex forms of communication, such as prompting entire communities to leave nest sites in search of new ones. And many insects use pheromones as sexual attractants.

Mammals, including humans, make some use of pheromones as well. When deer hunters speak of pheromones, they are talking about volatile substances in the urine or glandular secretions of deer that prompt bucks to chase does for breeding. In addition, some biologists theorize that pheromones in the urine or glandular secretions of bucks actually prompt does to come into estrous, influencing the timing, intensity, and duration of the rut.

If we think of deer as having a sort of wireless communication, we're probably not too far off the mark. Between urine and various glandular secretions released into the air and deposited in scrapes and rubs, deer are in near-constant contact with one another. Scent keeps them aware of the deer living in the area, as well as any deer passing through, and conveys information about the age,

It is often true that a rub made on a large tree is probably made from a larger racked buck. The opposite, however, is not always true as evidenced by the sapling that this 12-point buck is rubbing. CREDIT TED ROSE.

This hunter is creating a false rub. Instinctively, bucks will be quick to check out new rubs in their area. Don't forget to add scent! CREDIT FIDUCCIA ENTERPRISES.

general health, social position, and breeding status. Scent probably also tells them something about where other deer have been and what they've been eating.

For hunters, the question is, how can we plug into this communications network ourselves and use it to help us find deer, lure deer into shooting range, or develop a successful hunting strategy? ■

PLAY THE WIND

It's a simple enough concept: stay downwind of the game. Few hunters are so confident in their scent-reduction routine that they believe they can totally ignore the wind. And no matter how religiously we follow our routines, as a practical matter it is sometimes impossible to get to a hunting spot from cabin, home, or vehicle without picking up foreign smells somewhere along the way. For hunters in remote areas, hunting from wall tents or spike camps, showering is not usually an option–nor is avoiding smoke, cooking smells, or the odors from fuel, oil, gunpowder, cleaning solvents, and a variety of other odiferous items. The most successful hunters I know, including those who believe in reducing scent as much as possible, nonetheless always take the wind into consideration in planning their hunting strategies. Most of them will not consider hunting a given stand when the wind direction is wrong for that stand. In fact, most of them will get out of a stand and move to another location if they're in a stand and the wind changes direction. They are convinced that this careful attention to wind direction is a key to their success, and that attention to wind direction may well be one of the most important distinguishing factors between consistently successful hunters and those who rarely see a mature buck.

Simple as the concept of staying downwind can be, applying it requires knowledge, scouting, and careful planning. Whether hunting from a stand, still hunting, or even driving deer, wind direction is important. First, though, it's necessary to understand the wind itself, and how prey animals relate to it.

Deer play the wind, and hunters should, too. This bedded buck lies with cover and the wind at his back. He can see anything approaching across the open field, smell (and hear) anything approaching from behind.

Hunters who think using the wind is as simple as holding up a wet finger are going to get busted again and again. Unfortunately, it's not that simple, and hunters need to understand prevailing breezes, how terrain affects wind direction, and thermals.

Most hunters are aware of a prevailing breeze in their area. In much of the county, prevailing breezes come from the southwest. North America has the distinction of owning one of the most volatile and violent climates in the world, largely because the prevailing breezes in much of the country pick up energy and moisture from the Gulf of Mexico, spawning torrential rainstorms and sometimes tornados that make their way north and east.

Still, a southwesterly prevailing breeze simply means that, on a given day, the wind is more likely to come from the southwest than from any other direction. There are still days on which it comes from other directions. Not only that, it shifts, as anyone who has ever tried to dodge the smoke from a campfire has learned. (Yes, sitting close to a campfire can create something of a vacuum or an eddy that will seem to draw the smoke, but there is no getting around the fact that wind direction often shifts.)

What's more complicated is the way the terrain–hills, ridges, valleys, trees, and even big rocks–affects wind direction. The best analogy might be water flowing in a stream. There is a prevailing current, but the water flows more slowly near the banks than in the deeper parts of the stream. Turns in the course of the stream, along with rocks, deadfalls, sandbars, and other structures cause eddies, where the current swirls and even flows against the prevailing direction. At the foot of a falls, a hydraulic is created, sometimes for the width of the stream. Water drops over the falls and goes down, then rises and flows back toward the falls, to recirculate. Buoyant objects including, tragically, people, can be caught in these circular flows indefinitely.

Air currents travel in much the same way over the landscape, flowing around and over obstacles, turning and sometimes flowing in the opposite direction. Eddies are formed in some places, where the air currents circle continuously.

As you might imagine, a hunter in an area in which the air is swirling continuously is likely to be picked off by any game animal that moves through that area. Smart hunters avoid such areas, and some successful hunters locate their stands at or near the top of hills, or in large expanses of flat country, for that reason. Air currents do differ from water in a stream, though, because the water in a stream predictably flows in the same general direction. The extent to which air currents swirl or eddy is dependent upon the direction of the wind at any given time. A stand in a given valley may be impossible to hunt effectively when prevailing breezes blow, but a properly positioned stand might be a good spot on a day when the wind blows consistently straight down the length of the valley.

An odorless powder like this will help you detect prevailing, thermal, and the most troublesome of currents, a deflective or convection current while you are on stand.

One great illustration of the fact that the terrain affects wind direction, often dramatically, can be observed by anyone at a long-range muzzleloader shooting event. Any bullet can be affected by wind, but the relatively lower velocities achieved by most muzzleloaders makes the wind an even bigger factor. At serious shoots, flags will be placed at regular intervals of ten or twenty yards so that shooters can dope the wind and adjust their aim accordingly. It's not unusual to see a twenty-yard flag blowing left to right while the flags at 80 yards and beyond blow right to left.

Deer make use of the wind, and prefer to travel in a way that puts it to their advantage. Still, if deer only traveled into the wind, they'd all wind up in the same location eventually. They travel into it when they can, but they also use a quartering wind, and will travel with the wind when the food source, bedding area, or other objective is downwind from them. Mature deer, in particular, tend to travel along the downwind side of fields, forest openings, or any potential source of danger, and they will often circle downwind of anything suspicious they become aware of. They don't use the wind exclusively for safety, though. They also use it to keep tabs on one another, and bucks are famous for scent-checking trails, food sources, scrapes, and bedding areas, often moving along downwind of these areas when looking for does as the rut approaches.

Hunting to take advantage of the wind becomes something of a chess match, with deer attempting to use it to their advantage as hunters do the same thing. Given the superiority of the whitetail's nose, this is a battle the hunter is usually going to lose, but if he doesn't play the game well, it's a battle he will almost always lose.

WIND AND STAND HUNTING

It's often said that if deer were predictable hunters would kill them all, and that is true enough. On the other hand, their movements are far from random. They travel between food sources and bedding areas. They travel to water. Bucks travel to find does, and under certain conditions, vice versa. All else being equal, they take the path of least resistance, but all else is seldom equal. Their routes are strongly influenced by safety (they avoid open areas, particularly mature deer and particularly during daylight hours), and by hills, streams, roads, etc.

The serious hunter puts up multiple stands which will be hunted at various times depending on the date as well as the time of day, or he uses portable stands such as lightweight hang-ons, or climbers, to access the various feeding areas, bedding areas, or travel routes. Most successful hunters, especially bow hunters, look for choke points that tend to funnel deer movement.

This stand was placed with the prevailing breeze on the downwind side of where the deer most often come to the field. CREDIT FIDUCCIA ENTERPRISES.

One way to play the wind is to simply consider the prevailing breeze and hang a stand on the downwind side of the area through which the hunter expects the deer to travel. It's important, as we mentioned earlier, to look at the terrain and consider the possibility of eddies and other irregularities in the air currents. An educated guess can usually be made with a quick look around, but the only way to be certain is to get into the stand and test the air with Windfloaters, or a similar item designed to indicate wind direction. (Milkweed pods work very well for this, by the way. Pick them in the fall and put them in plastic sandwich bags, then take a pod or two along in your day-pack when hunting.) Wind checkers of this sort can reveal some real surprises, sometimes blowing right to left for 15 feet, dropping a few feet, and suddenly changing directions. In some cases they will take off at a certain height and travel a great distance in a totally unpredicted direction.

Bowhunters who stalk game often tie a feather to their quiver or some other accessory. The feather will indicate the presence and the direction of even the slightest puff of wind. That won't work in a tree stand, though, for the just-stated reason that the air is not necessarily blowing in the same direction at ground level as it is 15 or 20 feet up a tree. Those differences in wind direction at various heights may be one reason why a deer that seems to be directly downwind of a hunter doesn't catch his scent or, conversely, why a deer a hunter thought was upwind did catch his scent.

Hanging a stand on what is normally the downwind side of the trail only works, of course, when prevailing breezes blow. That stand must be avoided at

Field & Stream Deputy Editor, Jay Cassell, always checks the wind several times during his stalk into his stand as well as during his post. Some of the commercially available non-scented powders have white powder, others have orange-colored powder. CREDIT FIDUCCIA ENTERPRISES.

other times, which can be a limiting factor. It takes discipline to stay away from a good spot because the wind is wrong. There is another option. If the spot is that hot, the hunter can hang two stands, on opposite sides of the trail, funnel, or area through which the deer are expected to travel, hunting whichever stand is on the downwind side on a given day.

Wind direction is only one factor to consider when selecting a stand site. Another is thermals. Strictly defined, a thermal is a rising current of warm air, but hunters tend to use the term more loosely to refer to the fact that warm air tends to rise, while cooling air falls. It is probably not a big factor on breezy days, but becomes a huge factor when there is no discernible wind. Thermals can affect the hunter in a number of ways. In hilly terrain, for instance, as the sun rises in the morning and the temperature climbs, air will tend to move uphill. In the afternoon, when temperatures begin to drop, air will flow downhill. Consider a stand near the top of a hill, perched uphill from a bench or a hillside trail below. In the morning, when rising air currents lift the air toward the hilltop, it's an excellent stand. Later in the afternoon, as dropping temperatures send the air rolling downhill, it's a terrible stand.

In a flatter area, rising air currents might lift a hunter's scent beyond the range of deer approaching from any direction, but falling temperatures (again, with no wind) can carry the hunter's scent straight down to the base of the tree, where it may spread out in all directions. It's bad news, especially for the bowhunter, when the Windfloaters drop slowly to the ground immediately below.

Height, too, can be a factor. Many hunters argue that 10 or 12 feet is adequate, and 15 feet is a very common height for ladder stands. Still, most of the more successful hunters I know prefer to be closer to 20 feet, with some preferring 25 feet or more. To begin with, if height doesn't matter, why are we climbing trees at all? Some hunters would argue–and I'm inclined to agree–that a hunter is better off on the ground than at a height of 10 or 12 feet. At reduced heights, the hunters is more exposed than on the ground, while at the same time being well within the peripheral vision of any deer at ground level. With regard to scent, it isn't hard to imagine that under the right conditions, a breeze can carry the scent of a hunter over the head of deer passing close to the stand–assuming the hunter is high enough.

None of this is to suggest that hunters should venture up to heights at which they're uncomfortable. Safety is paramount, and a nervous hunter is more prone to accidents. Personally, I'm not comfortable at heights over twenty feet. I try to get as close to 20 feet as I can, though, because my experience has been that I get picked off less frequently at heights around 20 feet than I do at heights of 12 or 15 feet, whether because I'm spotted or because my scent is picked up.

Hunters who are uncomfortable at heights of at least 15 feet will want to take extra precautions in positioning their stands, both in terms of scent control, playing the wind, providing adequate concealment, remaining as motionless as possible, and wearing good head-to-toe camo, including face masks or camo paint and gloves.

The Deer Box is an ideal lightweight ground blind that can be heated in the winter. This blind helps to keep your scent from deer even though you are at ground level. This unique blind comes with a built-in lock, an inside digital thermometer and clock, and has noise-free windows that open inwards. CREDIT FIDUCCIA ENTERPRISES.

Another option, of course, is a good ground blind. Conceivably, fully enclosed ground blinds can contain scent to some degree. More and more blinds are being manufactured with a layer of activated carbon to adsorb scent. Scent reducing products can be sprayed on those that lack carbon. Naturally ground blinds should be stored in areas where they are unlikely to be contaminated with the smell of gasoline, engine exhaust, paints or paint thinners, or smoke. Ideally, they'll be set up in position at least a few days prior to their use, to dissipate any smells they may have absorbed.

Not too many years ago–well within my memory, I'm afraid–hunters ventured into the woods without benefit of tree stands or manufactured ground blinds. They walked to their spot and sat, or stood, against a tree, watching for game. Few bowhunters still use this approach, but quite a few gun hunters do. In many cases they're placed ahead of hunters who are driving deer, but whatever the circumstances these hunters need to give special attention to reducing scent and playing the wind.

STILL HUNTING

While deer drives are common in certain areas, still hunting is practiced by some hunters anywhere there are deer to hunt. Effective still hunters usually move at a snail's pace, but even moving slowly, mobility gives them the opportunity to take maximum advantage of the wind. Assuming they've scouted the area, they can, and should, plan a route that will allow them to approach trails, funnels, food sources, or bedding areas from a downwind (or quartering) position. Deer, especially mature ones, tend to keep a careful eye out downwind, knowing they are vulnerable from that direction. Big bucks are notorious for bedding near the end of points positioned in such a way that the wind is at their back, warning them of any predator approaching from that direction, while they can see for some distance to their downwind side. Still, defeating the eyes of any deer is considerably less challenging than defeating its nose.

Still hunters, no less than stand hunters, need to be aware of the effects of terrain on wind direction, as well as thermals and other factors. Bowhunters, as we mentioned, often attach a piece of dental floss or a feather to a quiver or bow as a wind indicator; gun hunters, especially when still hunting, would do well to follow suit, or to use milkweed seeds or a commercially available wind detector, to keep tabs on changing wind directions.

DEER DRIVES

Deer drives are one scenario in which many hunters give little thought to wind direction. After all, making deer aware of the presence of drivers is usually one of the objectives, the plan being that deer will move past a hunter waiting along an escape route. Many hunters on drives move through the woods making as much noise as possible, but that may not be the most effective way to drive deer.

Safety is paramount, and always merits extra consideration on a drive. That factor, and the layout of the area in terms of terrain and cover, can some-times make it difficult to use the wind to advantage. All else being equal,

A hunter took this Ohio buck still-hunting through an oak glade.

This Kentucky whitetail was taken on a river-bottom drive.

though, there are some advantages in having drivers move downwind, in the direction of hunters standing along the expected escape routes. When drivers move quietly, with the wind at their back, deer tend to pick up the scent of the drivers from some distance. They know they are in the area, and possibly approaching, but they don't panic–they simply move out ahead of them, occasionally looking back. The result is that shooters have a greater chance of seeing deer that are moving slowly, occasionally stopping, as opposed to racing at full speed. Few deer hunters practice shooting at moving targets enough to shoot ethically at a deer running at top speed.

Flankers on the drive, too, are more likely to have good shooting opportunities at deer attempting to sneak around behind the drivers when this approach is used.

While playing the wind in this manner can be advantageous on any drive, it can be particularly useful for hunters whose numbers are limited. Assuming adequate scouting, careful planning, and a knowledge of how deer use the local terrain, three, two, or even a single driver can zig-zag downwind slowly to effectively move deer past a hunter waiting downwind.

FUNNELING DEER WITH SCENT

Some might consider it a risky strategy–and it is–but more than one bowhunter has intentionally used human scent to funnel deer and put them in shooting range. By strategically hanging recently worn socks or tee-shirts from fence posts or trees, savvy hunters can sometimes steer deer in their direction, causing them to skirt downwind of travel lanes, or choose one trail or choke point over another travel route. Gun hunters are less likely to avail themselves of this strategy, since they can cover much larger areas, but for the frustrated bowhunter who knows bucks are moving through an area but can't quite seem to get within bow range, such a strategy might make the difference. It's not a strategy to try, though, without a thorough knowledge of how the deer travel through a given area. ■

SCENT REDUCTION

Let me begin by admitting a bias up front. I am highly doubtful of the notion that scent can be eliminated. The real question, as I see it, is not if scent can be eliminated, but if it can be reduced sufficiently to give hunters an advantage they would not otherwise have.

Answering that question is difficult for several reasons. Little truly independent research has been done on the subject. Scent, as we have seen, is a matter of volatile (gaseous) molecules being carried through the air to the sensory organs, usually nasal passages, of an animal. While the technology and methodology may exist to determine the concentration of these molecules in a given controlled area, few independent labs with the necessary resources have to date had sufficient motivation to conduct the kind of research that would provide useful information to hunters. Further complicating things, hunters are dealing with biology and uncontrolled conditions, not machines in a lab. A machine may indicate the concentration of various molecules in an enclosed space, but that does not tell us how those molecules behave in a forest or on a prairie. It also doesn't tell us at what level of concentration a given species under given circumstances can detect those molecules, or how they will react to various concentrations of them.

What we are left with then, is common sense and anecdotal evidence accumulated by hunters in the field. (Another bias: I'm highly skeptical of common sense. Common sense would suggest the sun circles the earth. Science tells us it's the other way around, and I'm inclined to go with science.)

Anecdotal evidence is far from perfect, but it is evidence and should not be ignored. And anecdotal evidence suggests that scent reduction can make a difference. Virtually every consistently successful deer hunter I know makes some effort to reduce or control scent in some way. Somewhere out there, I'm sure, is a consistently successful hunter who pays no attention to scent control. I just haven't met him. Imperfect though the evidence may be, thousands upon thousands of hunters who have logged countless hours in tree stands and blinds have come to the conclusion that taking some measures to reduce scent while afield is worth the effort and the expense.

When hunters talk about controlling odor, they are talking about two things. One is the odor produced continuously by their bodies and their breath. (Or more specifically, by various secretions and the action of bacteria on these secretions.) The other involves the various odors with which they or their clothing and gear may be contaminated, including soaps and shampoos, shaving creams, lotions, ointments, smoke, gas fumes, oils, mothballs, foods and beverages, cooking odors, and any other substance that hunters or their gear may come in contact with. We can speculate about which of these odors are more important, and which of these odors animals may or may not associate with humans or with danger, but the simplest and safest course of action for any hunter concerned about scent control is to try and keep all odors to an absolute mini- mum. Knowing how best to do this requires a basic understanding of how various scent reduction products work.

STARTING CLEAN

While it may be possible to reduce scent, it seems only reasonable to start out with as little scent as possible. That means on our person, on our clothing, and on our gear. Commercial soaps and detergents are usually scented, and most leave behind a residue. Fortunately, the shelves of most sporting goods stores, and the pages of most hunting catalogs, are well stocked with a variety of commercially produced soaps, detergents, shampoos, and underarm deodorants, all unscented and promising to leave behind little or no residue. There are even unscented cleaners and deodorants for boots.

Brushing teeth and gargling, while it won't eliminate breath odors, can keep down the bacteria that contribute to these odors.

Many hunters watch their diets before heading for the woods, avoiding strong smelling foods such as onions and garlic. These not only affect the breath, but their odors can be detected in perspiration. Finally, some hunters

A savvy hunter washes prior to each hunt in order to remove any bodily or foreign odors that deer may detect. CREDIT IN-SCENTS.

advocate taking zinc to reduce body odor.

Properly stored, much of our gear is less likely to be odiferous, one exception being our guns and bows, more specifically the solvents and lubricants we use on them. Best bet here is to use as much of these products as needed, but avoid using excessive amounts. There are, by the way, lubricants on the market advertised as having little or no scent, and there are others with cover scents, such as pine scent.

AVOIDING CONTAMINATION

At its most basic level, scent reduction means avoiding contamination by foreign scents. When it comes to clothing, that can be as simple as storing clean hunting clothes in a sealed bag or container of some sort, assuming of course that the container itself does not emit an odor. It also means avoiding contamination before and after storage to the extent possible. Many hunters like to dry their clothes outdoors, for instance, to avoid possible contamination from fabric softeners that have been used in a dryer. That's fine, unless your neighbor upwind fires up his grill or his wood stove while the clothes are drying.

Hanging gear in the garage between hunts is a habit I'm working to avoid. The fabric seats and the straps on climbing stands, along with blinds and other items, will surely absorb exhaust fumes and the other odors associated with vehicles. Better to store gear in an unattached shed, if possible. Not all sources of contamination are that obvious, though.

I recently watched in amazement as a hunting buddy of mine, who uses a variety of scent control products on his clothing, climbed into my truck on the way to a hunt and casually lit up a cigarette. I'm not amazed that he smokes, or that he might have decided he'd rather smoke than remain scent free–I'm amazed that he bothers with the expense and effort of reducing scent, then contaminates his clothing and gear with smoke.

Stopping by the diner for breakfast while wearing hunting clothes is

When keeping your hunting clothes outside, be sure they are away from the outside dryer vent and away from the grill (if you happen to fire it up for some tasty grilled venison steaks). CREDIT FIDUCCIA ENTERPRISES.

another source of contamination. And how many hunters stop at the gas station en route to their hunting spot? If gas fumes don't contaminate their clothes, how about the puddles of gas and oil they're tromping around in that will undoubtedly adhere to the soles of their boots?

To the hunter trying hard to keep such scent contamination to a minimum, the entire world suddenly becomes one big source of unwanted odors, some of which catch him by surprise. Stopping to pick up a hunting buddy on a recent outing (the same one who smokes), I found him under the hood of his car squirting a lubricant on his fan belt. Remembering a squeaky clutch peddle that was beginning to drive me nuts, I grabbed the spray lubricant when he set it down, leaned under my dash, and sprayed it on the peddle. Big mistake. Instantly the entire inside of my vehicle, and presumably everything in it, smelled like kerosene.

The best way to keep such incidental odors to a minimum is to keep the hunting clothes and boots in their air tight container, and change after exiting the vehicle, at the location of the hunt. At first I considered this a huge bother. Over time, though, it has become a habit I would stick with even if I weren't concerned about scent control. I've discovered that I'm much more comfortable driving, on the way to and especially from a hunt, in street clothes and shoes. Given that, keeping my hunting clothes in a sealed container becomes a convenient way to keep them together and organized, in addition to helping avoid scent contamination.

SCENT REDUCTION PRODUCTS

Assuming we're as clean as possible, the next step is to recognize that we cannot get entirely scent-free, and even if we could that condition would not last long. That's where scent reducing products come in. To understand which ones to use and when, it's necessary to understand how the various scent reducing products work, and what they are designed to do.

Essentially, there are three types of commercially produced products intended to reduce odors. These are 1) products designed to prevent the formation of certain odors, by killing or inhibiting the growth of bacteria that cause these odors, or by neutralizing acidity 2) products designed to prevent the formation of the gas molecules that form odors, and 3) products with activated carbon that adsorb odors.

Sodium bicarbonate—more commonly referred to as baking soda—is famous for its ability to control odors by neutralizing acids, including the acids present in perspiration. It is the active ingredient in a number of the scent control products being marketed to hunters. If the product suggests that you can gargle with it, odds are the active ingredient is baking soda. The best way to use many of these products is to apply them directly to the skin after showering. Apply them everywhere, if you like, but pay special attention to the areas that perspire the most.

Plain baking soda can be useful, either as a deodorant (mix it with a little corn starch to keep it from clumping), as a toothpaste, or a mouth rinse. For hunters who cannot (or prefer not) to line-dry clothes, a few tablespoons of baking soda in the dryer can dry them scent free.

Another product that acts in a similar fashion is silver in clothing fabric. Silver has long been known for its antimicrobial properties. (In plain language, it kills germs.) The U.S. army has for some time issued to infantrymen socks with silver in the fabric to control the growth of bacteria that give rise to a number of foot ailments. In more recent years, at least one maker of hunting garments offers socks and undergarments including silver. The idea is to prevent the growth of the bacteria that cause body odors.

Stopping odors by controlling the conditions that create them is one approach; another approach entails a chemical interaction with substances to prevent volatility. As we have seen, odors are formed when substances release molecules into the atmosphere. Some substances are not volatile. Steel, for instance, is not volatile and normally has no odor. A chemical reaction that controls volatility–that is, one that stops the release of molecules into the air–prevents odors. Many of the scent reduction products that are sprayed onto the skin, clothing, or gear, operate on this principle. The disadvantage of these products is that they are in effect consumed as they function, and must be regularly re-applied to continue working

Finally, among the more recent means of scent control for hunters is the use of carbon-impregnated clothing. Any hunter who has looked at an ad for these garments probably has a basic understanding of how they work. Tiny carbon granules trap and hold odor molecules, preventing their release into the air. Eventually the granules are full up, and can contain no more odor molecules. An application of heat releases some, if not all of these molecules, freeing the carbon granules to trap odors again.

The use of activated carbon has long had industrial and military applications, usually for controlling or neutralizing toxic substances of various kinds. The military often issues carbon clothing to personnel in areas where there is the threat of chemical weapons. It works.

The use of carbon clothing for odor control is more controversial. In industrial applications, carbon that has adsorbed its capacity and will be re-used is heated at temperatures that would destroy any garments. The argument is often made that the temperatures to which carbon clothing is exposed in a clothes dryer are insufficient to achieve the desired results. The case made by the manufacturers of these garments is that heat at these temperatures, while it may not entirely eliminate the scent molecules trapped by the carbon, will eliminate enough of them to enable the garment to work as intended.

In the only truly scientific study of scent control I have found–at least as it might have some relevance to a hunting situation–Dr. John Shivik of the National Wildlife Research Center extensively tested the ability of seven search dogs to find people wearing scent-control clothing, compared to their ability to locate people not wearing such clothing. The people were placed in blinds, the dogs were allowed to sniff a piece of fabric previously handled by the people in the blinds, and dogs and handlers were then given specified amounts of time in which to locate the subjects. In all but one of forty-two trials, dogs found all the test subjects within the allotted time. Dr. Shivik found that persons not wearing carbon suits were detected from slightly greater distances, but did not find the differences in distance to be statistically significant. While noting that he believed it possible for individuals to put on sealed carbon suits in such a way as to remain undetectable to dogs, his overall conclusion was that for practical purposes, carbon suits are ineffective.

In fairness, if we are going to be truly scientific in our approach, we have to concede that the results of one test are never conclusive. It will be interesting to see if other researchers can duplicate these results, or if they arrive at different conclusions. As a side note, it is significant (though not surprising) that Shivik did observe significant differences in the time it took dogs to find subjects, and these differences were related to barometric pressure, humidity, and the variability of the wind. Shivik also speculated that one probable source of contamination of the suits was that wearers handled them in putting them on. Hunters using these suits might want to consider wearing rubber gloves when donning them.

BLINDS

Blinds haven't traditionally been thought of as scent reduction products, so I've given them their own category. When I say "traditionally," I mean that few hunters would associate blinds with reductions in scent–but that's not to say the thought has never occurred to hunters. In recent years, with the growing popularity of commercially produced, fully enclosed blinds, a number of hunters have suggested that these blinds could help contain scent. Use of such ground blinds is increasing in popularity, but they have not been commonly used long enough to accumulate the kind of anecdotal evidence that has built up around other scent reducing products, like the clothing and soaps.

Still, it doesn't seem inconceivable that blinds could afford some degree of scent control, if only because they block the wind, thereby preventing it from carrying at least some scent downwind. More recently, some blind makers have been offering in blinds the same carbon-impregnated fabrics that are offered in hunting garments. Clearly these are designed to be scent reduction products, and are one more weapon to consider in the arsenal of hunters committed to achieving every possible edge they can get in the effort to defeat the nose of a whitetail.

Arguably the ultimate in scent-control is the Deluxe Blind from

This blind from Scentite help to reduce human scent and include a vent pipe that extends from the ceiling of the blind up 30 feet (where most times it is secured to a limb of a tree). CREDIT FIDUCCIA ENTERPRISES.

SCENTite. Essentially, this blind is a large, air-tight box that vents scent thirty feet above the blind–assuming the blind is on the ground–and higher than that if the blind is on a quad stand. SCENTite owner Bill Ferguson demonstrates its effectiveness by creating smoke inside the blind. The blind does indeed completely contain the smoke, letting none of it out until it reaches the top of the vent tube at least 30 feet up.

Bill's observations using this blind not only demonstrate its effectiveness, but result in some observation about scent and how it is carried that might have a more general application.

"Some common sense has to be used in terms of blind placement and current conditions," Bill explains. "For instance, if you're in a valley and deer are traveling downwind around the hillside at a height of 30 feet or more, they will probably pick up the scent of the hunter in the blind. As far as we've been able to observe, though, a hunter in a more or less flat area, or on or near a hilltop, will remain undetected by deer in his hunting area. Getting the scent up at least 25 feet seems to carry it over the heads of any deer in the area until it dissipates."

What about downdrafts?

"Honestly," says Bill, "the only situation in which I've seen deer detect scent from this blind is when they are on a hillside above it. I have not yet seen deer that were below the level of the vent detect hunters in the blind. In fact, after the season we've often put a line of corn all the way around the blind about five feet out, and had deer come in and eat all the way around with two people inside the blind. We do that just to demonstate its effectiveness."

The more serious hunters I know tend to employ at least some of the scent-reduction strategies outlined in this chapter, and many use them all. They wash themselves and their clothing in unscented soaps and detergents, store their garments carefully in sealed containers, use scent-reducing products, and in many cases wear carbon clothing. Few totally ignore wind direction.

My own experiences, which I present here as neither less nor more valid than those of any other experienced hunter, are inconclusive. Depending on circumstances, I use some or all of these products. I have been detected by game when following a rigid scent control regimen. I have also had game downwind of me for extended periods of time, and remained undetected.

In addition I have observed, as have many hunters, that game animals at times appear to detect an odor, but not to a degree that causes them to bolt. The head comes up, perhaps, and they appear to change from a relaxed state to a

Many hunters believe enclosed ground blinds can help contain scent. Some blinds make use of carbon-impregnated fabrics to adsorb scent. The blind above is the Baby Brickhouse from Ameristep.

tense state. They look around, as if looking for the source of a faint odor. It could be that they detect an odor, but think it is at some distance, or are simply unable to locate the source of it. I've even had deer snort, or jump and run a short distance, only to stop. On more than one occasion I've had the opportunity to arrow animals that I'm sure were aware of my presence, but couldn't locate me. It is not unreasonable to speculate in these situations that keeping scent to a minimum is the difference between an animal that becomes alert to possible danger and remains in the area long enough to provide a shooting opportunity, and one that bolts instantly.

Based on all this, I am inclined to continue using scent reducing strategies unless and until more extensive scientific studies convince me they are ineffective. My thinking, which appears to be in accord with the thoughts of many experienced hunters, is that getting within range of mature big game animals is sufficiently difficult that I want any edge I can get. ■

ATTRACTANT SCENTS

My friend Rick Dunn was toting his slug gun down a logging road on a farm in south-central Ohio, stopping periodically to apply a few drops of doe-in-heat scent to the pad on his boot. He had only a vague destination in mind, and no particular strategy beyond the use of the scent trail he was laying down. Rick is a high-energy type, and a little on the restless side, and he had spent as many hours sitting in a tree stand as he could tolerate in one day.

He had covered maybe half-a-mile on the long, winding dirt road, and had stopped once again to apply the doe urine, when he caught movement from the corner of his eye. Something was traveling down the logging road behind him, and since the road made a big, winding path, he was catching just glimpses of it through the woods. He stepped off the road, behind a tree, to watch. Eventually it came around the bend and he could see it clearly–a big-racked buck, nose to the ground, following his trail like a hound after a rabbit.

Rick's too experienced a hunter to waste time in a situation like that. He shouldered his gun, put the crosshairs on the sweet spot, and squeezed off a shot. Not long after, he was field dressing his big Ohio buck. And as you might imagine, Rick is sold on the use of doe-in-heat scent when deer hunting, at least when he's hunting close to or during the rut.

There is no question that deer can be lured into shooting position with scents. What is equally clear is that scent doesn't always work. And when it does work, just why is a controversial issue in the case of many scents.

Of course, anything that always worked would have to be illegal. Hunters aren't really looking for something that always works. They're looking for something that gives them an edge–something that makes the odds against scoring on any given day a little lower. How many times would you use scent for one opportunity at a good buck?

The issues for hunters are, what kind of scents work, when do they work, when (and why) do they often not work?

Attractant scents can be divided into several categories, though there may be some overlap. These are Food Scents, Sex Scents, and Curiosity Scents. Urine can also be a category of its own. Though it is often considered a sex scent, and might also be considered a curiosity scent, we'll explain why we list it as a category of its own later in this chapter.

Why do I say there may be some overlap among these categories? Until we can get inside a deer's head, we really have no way of knowing for certain what motivates it. Was it hungry and fooled by that bottled apple scent, or was it curious about a strange new smell it had never encountered before? Was that rutting buck fooled by the doe-in-heat scent, or was it curious about something that vaguely resembled the scent of a doe-in-heat but wasn't? Some would argue that any time deer respond to a bottled or synthesized scent, they are responding mostly from curiosity. And of course some hunters would say, "Who cares why they come in, just so they come in?"

Manufacturers themselves recognize the overlap. Many refer to their scents as lures. The ingredients are something they prefer to keep secret, but they often indicate that the lure contains a mixture of ingredients designed to appeal to hunger, or curiosity, or both.

FOOD SCENTS

First let's distinguish between "food" and "food scents." In states such as Michigan or Texas, where baiting deer is perfectly legal, hunters may put corn, apples, beets, or similar foods out as bait, and it seems reasonable to assume deer that encounter the bait for the first time are responding to smell.

That is not what we are talking about by use of food scents, however. By "food scents" in this context we are talking about the use of bottled scents made from concentrates or synthetic odors, or solid mixtures that are volatile enough to produce food scents that can be detected from some distance, or various

Try using apple scent even in an area where there are no apples. A deer's natural curiosity may cause it to come in to check out the new food scent. CREDIT IN-SCENTS.

products that are heated or even boiled to produce scents intended to resemble foods.

An interesting issue related to food scents is the oft-heard caution about using the scents of foods that do not occur naturally in a given area. The idea is that a deer who suddenly detects the scent of, say, apples, in an area where there are no apple trees, will react with suspicion, or will sense in some way that something is not right and will avoid the area.

Many biologists, and some hunters, scoff at that idea.

"The idea that a deer catches a whiff of corn in an area where there is no cornfield and is suddenly on the alert or suspicious that something is fishy, is just ridiculous." well-known whitetail expert Peter Fiduccia told me recently. "Deer are very wary, but they're not that complicated. They don't think that way. If it smells like something good to eat and they're hungry, they'll check it out."

We can speculate about why deer respond to certain foods at certain times, and others at other times, but ultimately it's something only the deer themselves know. Bottom line for many hunters, though, is that putting out a food scent is unlikely to do any harm, and can sometimes be the ticket to success.

CURIOSITY SCENTS

Deer are without question curious creatures, which is the idea behind curiosity scents. They investigate their environment, and one of their chief instruments of investigation is their nose. They've been referred to as one hundred pound noses that run around smelling everything in the woods. Given their curiosity, and their reliance on their noses, it's not surprising that deer will on occasion approach the source of a strong, unusual, or unknown aroma to check it out.

What exactly are curiosity scents? In the case of commercially produced scents, that is a difficult question, since manufacturers are highly secretive about the formulas they claim to have developed after years of study. In one University of Georgia study involving the use of motion-activated cameras placed over a variety of scents, the numbers of deer attracted to car polish rivaled the numbers attracted to several kinds of urine and food scents

SEXUAL ATTRACTANTS

Sexual attractants don't just get deer excited, they get hunters excited. No mystery there–when you consider that close to and during the rut is the one time when even big, secretive bucks allow their obsession with hot does to make them vulnerable, it's not surprising that hunters would seek to take advantage of that vulnerability. Probably the most commonly used sexual attractant is doe-in-heat urine, which may be placed on the ground, or used to saturate a rag or a wick and hung from a tree, or even sprayed into the air. Hunters also frequently use doe urine to lay down scent trails, saturating a rag that can be dragged, or a pad that can be worn on a boot sole.

Buck urine is most effectively used during the rut. Bucks high on the pecking order are quick to check out if the urine is from a buck they know, or a strange buck. CREDIT IN-SCENTS.

Dominant buck urine, too, is popular. The idea is that bucks detecting the scent of another buck in their area will feel challenged and will seek out the buck to chase it off. Still others theorize that dominant buck urine can attract and hold does in a given area. It has been demonstrated that does can determine the difference between subordinate and dominant bucks. Though we tend to think of the bucks as seeking the does, does will frequent areas containing

Peter Fiduccia discovered in the 1970s that using buck urine on a mock rub helps to complete the illusion, both visually and through the odor. CREDIT FIDUCCIA ENTERPRISES.

dominant bucks, and especially in those areas where the buck to doe ratio is in good balance, does may travel outside their home ranges to find dominant bucks.

Among the more serious trophy hunters I know are several who begin placing dominant buck scents in various forms throughout their hunting area, usually late in the summer, though sometimes earlier, and in one case year-round. The theory is that this brings more does in the area, and keeps them there, and in turn more bucks are drawn into that area as the rut approaches. (More about this approach in subsequent chapters.)

Earlier we suggested that urine could be considered a category in itself. Here is why: ungulates, including deer, tend to be fascinated by urine of any kind. It seems to be a means of communication within the species, but may also tell deer about other species, including predators, in the area. There is some controversy regarding how deer react to the urine of predators, but regardless of how they react, they do seem drawn to check out urine. Ordinary doe urine is a commonly used scent. Many hunters believe that it doesn't make sense to use doe-in-heat scent before any does are likely to be in heat, but there are some other reasons not to use it. One reason is that it tends to repel does. The hunter looking primarily to cull does from a local herd or put venison in the freezer probably doesn't want to repel does. Beyond that, some hunters theorize that does attract bucks, so why drive away does?

The whole issue of how deer react to human urine has generated the widest possible response from hunters. At one extreme are the hunters who use bottles or other devices to avoid contaminating their hunting location with the smell of human urine. At the other extreme are hunters who intentionally "contaminate" their stands sites with human urine, deposit human urine in scrapes, and even create mock scrapes with human urine, in the belief that it attracts deer.

A number of more or less scientific studies in recent year have studied deer response to a variety of scents. The studies aren't always conclusive, but they do tend to point in a couple of interesting directions. One of these is that deer herds confined in pens don't always react to smells the same way wild deer do. The other is that neither penned nor free-ranging deer appear to have strong aversions to human urine, and may exhibit some curiosity about it. Bottom line: human urine may or may not attract deer to some degree, but it doesn't seem to repel them. Leave the urine bottles at home and let fly from your tree stand if you want.

Deer communicate through the odor of their urine during the breeding season. A doe in estrus will leave urine with a very strong odor. Bucks who are in the prime of their breeding season and at a prime age, will also leave urine with a strong musky odor. CREDIT TED ROSE.

The fact is, various studies indicate that deer sometimes show a mild curiosity reaction to a variety of odors from all kinds of urine to oddities such as car wax. One thing hunters don't need a scientific study to confirm: a deer detecting the close proximity of a human or other predator will turn inside out getting away.

Urine is not the only way deer convey sexual messages to one another–various glandular secretions, such as those deposited by bucks on rubs, may serve a similar function, along with the tarsal glands. A buck in rut can be smelled, even by the inferior noses of humans, for some distance under the right conditions, and any hunter who has picked a buck up by the hind legs to lift him into a pick-up truck, or who has ridden in an SUV with a buck behind the seat, is intimately acquainted with that aroma. Various commercial producers have attempted to bottle or mimic tarsal gland scent, and more than a few hunters like to trim off the tarsal glands of a tagged buck, to use as a lure. Many hunters freeze them in plastic bags for repeated use.

PHEROMONES

We can't address the issue of sexual scents without taking a look at pheromones. Pheromones are organic chemical substances used by various species to communicate with one another, or to produce any of a number of instinctive responses. Many insects, in particular, are known to use pheromones heavily. Pheromones may enable an ant to tell its community the location of a food source, for instance, or allow a colony of bees to coordinate an exodus from a hive to establish a new colony elsewhere. They also stimulate sexual activity. Insects aren't the only species that make use of pheromones. Mammals do, also.

Hunters became very excited about pheromones, more specifically the volatile substances in rutting buck or doe-in-heat urine that produce sexual responses in deer. A buck detecting these pheromones will instinctively react to them, every time. Hunters first learning about pheromones thought that perhaps they had hit on the holy grail of deer hunting: a scent that would invariably cause any buck encountering it to come to the source of the pheromones. Their hopes were dashed, however, by another incontrovertible fact: after they're released by the deer these pheromones last for anywhere from 15 seconds to, at most, 6 minutes. They work for deer because deer produce fresh pheromones continuously.

As with most mammals in the animal kingdom, pheromones create instinctive responses in both bucks and does. CREDIT TED ROSE.

Does this mean that, as a practical matter, there is no such thing as, wht is commonly referred to "doe-in-heat" scent? Some experts would argue that that is indeed the case. Consider, though, that scientists have identified at least ninety-three substances in the urine of a doe in heat. It seems entirely possible that a buck can tell a doe is in heat (actually she is in estrus) even without the pheromones. Will a buck respond to a doe even if the pheromones aren't present? We can't say with any certainty, but experiences like those of my friend Rick Dunn suggest that a buck will at least sometimes follow a trail of "doe-in-heat" scent, regardless of what the ingredients may be, and regardless of whether or not it contains pheromones. ∎

COVER SCENTS

Unexploded land mines are a major problem in war-torn parts of the world, killing and maiming innocent people sometimes many years after conflicts have ended. Proving yet again they are man's best friend, dogs have been trained to sniff them out. They find, them, too–six inches or more under ground, having been buried for years.

That in itself is amazing enough, but considering that the dogs are trained to respond to the explosive materials, which are often encased in a molded, solid block of inert material such as plastic, the feat is even more amazing.

Now consider this: most scientists are of the opinion that white-tailed deer have olfactory capabilities at least matching those of most dogs and, in the opinion of some, exceeding those of dogs. It is not unreasonable to wonder if it is possible for a hunter to mask his scent sufficiently to fool the nose of a deer. It doesn't help that behavioral scientists have observed that white-tailed deer can distinguish between as many as twenty different scents simultaneously.

Before you give up on the idea of cover scents, though, you might want to ponder this question: Why do some dogs seem to delight in rolling in the foulest, rottenest, most disgusting carcasses or other odiferous odors they can find? Biologists tell us that this behavior is common to wild as well as domesticated canines, and theorize that the behavior is an attempt to mask scent, as an aid in stalking prey.

Along similar lines, why do canines, felines, and other critters often kick dirt over their droppings, if not to reduce or mask scent?

Under the right conditions, hunting from a tree stand can carry scent over the heads of nearby game.

If we are correct in assuming that animals engage in these behaviors to reduce scent, then thousands upon thousands of years of evolution would seem to support the notion that it is indeed possible to mask scent to a degree that will make a hunter less easily detected by his prey. While it seems unlikely that scent can be entirely eliminated in this manner, perhaps it can be reduced to such a degree that it cannot be detected for as great a distance, or as quickly, by a prey species. Or perhaps the mixture of aromas causes a momentary hesitation, giving the predator a few extra seconds that can make the difference.

When camping or hunting from remote cabins, scent control can be a real challenge. When possible, leave outer garments outdoors on a porch or in a shed, where they won't pick up odors from fire, cooking, or other sources.

Native Americans were known to sometimes apply cover scents of one sort or another. Some tribes routinely sat in the smoke from campfires, convinced this cover scent gave them an edge when stalking into bow range of their quarry. They may not have understood scientific methodology, but they hunted almost daily all their lives, and for generation after generation depended on successful hunts for their very survival.

WHAT KIND OF COVER SCENT TO USE?

This is a more complicated question than it might at first appear to be. Typically, cover scents attempt to produce a strong smell that is common in the environment. Earth scent, pine scent, and the urine of common creatures such

Since foxes frequently inhabit the same areas that deer do, many hunters choose to use fox urine as a cover scent. CREDIT TED ROSE.

as foxes and raccoons are probably the most popular cover scents. Usually, earth and pine scents are sprayed on, or attached to an item of clothing in the form of wafers or patches, while urines are usually applied a few drops at a time to boot soles before entering the woods, to prevent deer from readily discerning the trail.

As in the case of food scents, some hunters feel it's important to use cover scents that are common to the area. In the case of fox or raccoon urine, there are few areas inhabited by deer that are not also inhabited by these critters. Dirt would seem to be a common element, though a hunter might wonder if a generic dirt scent would closely resemble everything from the red clay of Georgia, to the sand of the South Carolina Low Country, to the Arizona desert.

What about the use of urine from predators such as foxes? While some studies suggest that deer may react negatively to the urine of predators, other studies suggest otherwise. Then too, although the urine of various species may have different odors depending on what they have eaten, urine does tend to break down quickly in the environment to the point at which, according to some biologists, all mammal urine smells basically the same. Certainly many successful deer hunters routinely apply fox urine to their boots before entering the woods.

Still other hunters scoff at the notion that a deer is put on the alert by, for instance, the scent of pines in an area where there are no pine trees. My own take on this is that since it is as easy to use a scent that is common to the area being hunted as to use one that is not, why not use the locally common scent, just in case.

Here is another consideration: if half the hunters in the woods are using earth scent (or pine scent, or fox urine), might not a deer learn to associate that scent with hunters? In the West, many hunters, especially elk hunters, hunt from spike camps, where they usually spend at least some time sitting around campfires. More than one successful hunter has suggested the smell of smoke acts as an effective cover scent. In the introduction, I made reference to the hunters who smoke cigarettes on deer stands, putting a smoking butt in the fork of a tree just long enough to shoot an approaching deer, then finishing the smoke before climbing down to take up the trail. Could cigarette smoke be a cover scent?

Assuming cover scents can work, whether or not smoke (or any other scent) can act as a cover would probably depend upon whether or not deer have learned to associate the smoke, or other scents, with humans, and more specifically with danger. It seems unlikely that deer in a big woods, or a more or less remote

ATVs and similar vehicles enable hunters to cover ground without leaving scent. This is especially important when hunting trophy bucks, or when hunting the same area repeatedly.

area, would make that connection–although if they experience pain or a threat from one smoking hunter, the association could be made quickly. At the same time, deer that often come into contact with people, whether in heavily populated suburban areas, farm country, or areas where they are subject to heavy hunting pressure, would be quite likely to associate the smell of smoke with humans. ■

NATURAL VERSUS SYNTHETIC SCENTS

S cents of nearly any kind can be synthesized in laboratories. Are these inferior or superior to natural scents? Here are the arguments pro and con : On the pro side for synthetics, the argument is that certain substances, particularly urine, break down into other compounds, including ammonia. The ammonia smell is perfectly natural, and hence arguably a good thing. Soon after it is bottled, though, bacteria begin breaking urine down into unnatural compounds–unless special measures, including the use of preservatives, are used to prevent this. And preservatives, or so goes the argument, have their own unnatural scent. Synthetic scents, on the other hand, won't break down. And they're easier to use, since hunters needn't worry about when they were produced, or how they are stored, or how long they will be effective after the package is opened.

On the con side, some question whether or not it is possible to produce a synthetic scent that will fool a deer's nose. A deer will not have the same reaction, according to this line of reasoning, to a synthetic as opposed to a naturally produced scent. Any deer that respond to a synthetic scent, according to this position, are reacting out of curiosity, and not because they are genuinely fooled.

Here is another controversial issue concerning the use of natural urines: some products contain not deer urine but the urine of cattle or sheep. In fact, some doe-in-heat products actually contain the urine of cattle or sheep in heat. Hunters were scandalized to make that discovery, but it's not all that clear they

While deer do have set feeding patterns, they will often stop and browse as they move through an area. CREDIT TED ROSE.

should have been for one simple reason: deer respond to them, and no scientific evidence to date proves that the urine from real does in heat is more effective than the urine of other ungulates in heat.

Once again, we get into the motives of deer. Certainly the argument can be made that whether we truly fool a deer's nose or not, or whether they are reacting to a sexual stimulus or simply out of curiosity, doesn't matter. All that matters is, do they respond? To my knowledge no scientific studies have been completed regarding how deer react to natural versus synthetic scents, or fresh urine deposited by deer in the wild as compared to urine bottled on a deer farm and used weeks or months later.

TIMING

When is a good time to use scents? In the case of curiosity scents, arguably any time, since curiosity is not seasonal. Still, it seems unlikely a buck eagerly seeking a hot doe–or a doe being pursued by a randy buck–would stray far from its route to check a smell out of curiosity. At the same time, it seems unlikely a deer heading for a dinner of alfalfa, corn, or clover would delay getting dinner to check out a strange aroma. Nonetheless, any hunter who has spent time in the woods knows that deer aren't always chasing or being chased by other deer, nor are they always making a bee line for the nearest preferred food. Deer take their sweet time, most of the time, and tend to amble along slowly, browsing and grazing as they go.

When it comes to using food scents, timing raises some interesting and complex issues. As a general rule, most hunters, and even some manufacturers, recommend using food scents early in the season, pre-rut, and late in the season, post rut. Why? Because the period immediately before the rut, and during the peak of the rut, is prime time for doe-in-heat scents or dominant buck scents.

Again, to my knowledge, no one has done any sort of scientific (or for that matter unscientific) study to determine if doe-in-heat or dominant buck scents outperform food scents during the rut. Most manufacturers have little incentive to pursue such an inquiry; the status quo is that hunters use food scents on some hunts, sexual attractants on others. Why limit sales to one or the other?

How often have you heard that the best way to hunt bucks during the rut is to hunt where the does are? If that's sound advice, wouldn't it make perfect sense to attract does to your stand with food scents? Perhaps in some updated edition of this book, we'll have an answer to that question.

Corn is underrated as an important food source in November and December. Deer quickly make their way to a corn field to feed especially when the temperature goes below 28 degrees. CREDIT FIDUCCIA ENTERPRISES.

But the issue of when to use a given food scent is much more complicated than whether or not food scents are or are not more effective than sexual attractants at various times in the season. While it's true that deer like a variety of foods, it's also well documented that at any given time, deer have a preferred food, and will often pass up other foods to get to it. Further, their priorities change, sometimes from one day to the next. Deer may pass up any food source available to get at alfalfa in late summer or early autumn. Later they might switch to soybeans, passing up alfalfa to get the beans. When the acorns fall, deer will abandon every other food source to get to them. Though they readily eat the acorns from red oaks, they seem to prefer the less bitter white oak acorns

If there are wild apples in the area you are hunting, you can use apple scent as a cover scent. It would not make "scents" to use it as an attracting scent as the odor permeates the area from the natural ones on the trees. CREDIT FIDUCCIA ENTERPRISES.

given a choice. Why these changing preferences? Availability has something to do with it, but in many cases it's a matter of what is ripe. And some plants–especially broadleaf green plants such as the brassicas that are so popular these days in food plots–become sweeter after a frost or two, when they begin to die. They may literally be ignored one day, and sought after to the exclusion of nearly everything else the next day.

What does all this have to do with food scents? Neither corn scents or apple scents are likely to be at their most effective if acorns are dropping in the woods. And while all this might seem to suggest that acorn scents should be effective any time, there is the fact that deer seem to prefer foods with varying

Soybeans are also a favorite of deer. You have to plant at least a few acres in order to prevent deer from eating the plants before they sprout the beans. CREDIT FIDUCCIA ENTERPRISES.

Acorns are a crucial food source for whitetails, as they put a fat reserve on deer prior to the rut. Fertilizing oak trees twice a year helps them produce a healthier and more dependable mast crop. CREDIT TED ROSE.

One of the winter foods most sought by deer are turnips. Deer seek them out soon after the first heavy frost. Frigid Forage makes a Big N' Bold Brassica blend that includes turnips. Having food sources available late in the season will help keep the deer coming to your food plots. CREDIT FIDUCCIA ENTERPRISES.

amounts of protein or sugars depending on the time of the year and whether they are bulking up with protein or seeking high-energy foods with more sugars.

Timing as it pertains to the use of sexual scents would seem to be a more straightforward matter. Though there is some evidence that the scents released by bucks can actually stimulate does to come into heat, the timing of the rut is fairly predictable. A doe, as every deer hunter knows, will run from a buck until she is good and ready to stand still for him. At the same time, it is unlikely that bucks would respond to does in heat if not for the increased level of testosterone that courses through their veins as the rut kicks in. That would suggest that the best time to use dominant buck or doe-in-heat scent would be the period leading up to, and during, the time that the rut takes place, beginning when bucks begin frequently scraping, rubbing, and cruising for does, through the time when virtually all the does have been bred.

Earlier I made reference to some serious trophy hunters who begin making mock scrapes and putting out dominant buck scent in the summer, and sometimes year-round, in the belief that it attracts and holds does and bucks in an area. We'll take a closer look at that in a later chapter. ■

In this food plot, there are several crops planted to maintain the interest of the deer. The natural aroma of the sunflowers, corn, brassicas, and soybeans keep the deer coming to this spot on a regular basis. CREDIT FIDUCCIA ENTERPRISES.

SMELLING IS BELIEVING

I t was a gray, chilly, early November afternoon and I had been on stand about two hours. Bad weather and missed flight connections had delayed my arrival at Thunder Valley Outfitters in southern Iowa, and I had ended up getting into camp in the wee hours of the morning. I slept in, ate a late breakfast, and got to my stand about 12:30. Still tired from an entire day spent sitting in airports, and by my late arrival, I was nodding off periodically. The sound of dry leaves rustling snapped me out of my stupor, and I awoke to see a large, lone doe crossing not 15 yards in front of my stand, left to right–the same direction the wind was blowing. Given the date, and my guide's statement as he took me to my stand that he had seen no less than five bucks chasing does earlier that morning, I was naturally on the alert for the buck that was likely to be following her.

She walked by until she was directly downwind of me, and stopped, her attention suddenly riveted by the two Renzo's silhouette decoys I had put out, a bedded doe and a buck. She stared at them for half a minute, then began sneaking away, still downwind. About 80 yards out, she stopped, turned, and again stared at the decoys. Then began an entertaining series of head bobbings, stare downs, and hoof stomping, in an apparent effort to make the decoys move. For a good 20 minutes she stayed in the area, sometimes approaching the decoys, sometimes moving away from them. All the while I waited for her to catch my scent, snort, and run off, alerting any buck that was following her. Eventually she wandered off, but never got out of sight.

Fifteen minutes later, another doe came through. She moved off to my right, downwind, but I don't know if she spotted the decoys because my attention was fixed on the nice, symmetrical 140 class buck that soon came along behind her. I could hear her milling around, and again I was sweating bullets that she would catch my scent and bolt, taking her suitor with her.

He stopped briefly on the other side of a deadfall where I had no shot, but when the doe he was following moved off, he followed, moving quickly through two shooting windows. My grunts failed to stop him, and to my surprise he and the doe stopped downwind, about 80 yards out. I could just see the white tips of his antlers through the trees, while a little closer and further to my right, the other doe browsed contentedly.

Discouraged, I grunted aggressively in hopes of bringing him back. No luck. I grunted again, and heard an answering grunt from my left, along the same path the previous deer had taken. I grunted again and again heard an answering grunt, this one definitely closer. When the 160-class buck came into view I came to full draw, but he stopped in the same spot where the first buck had stopped, on the other side of the deadfall, perhaps a little further out.

This one spotted the decoys, though. He began grunting repeatedly, then put on a show of dominance, thrashing several small saplings. He was facing directly toward me, behind a thick mass of small limbs that I had no chance of getting an arrow through. When I could hold at full draw no longer, I let down as slowly and carefully as I could, my arms shaking with the effort. Probably because his attention was focused on the decoys, I got away with the movement.

For what seemed like a good ten minutes, the buck continued grunting and beating up the small saplings near the deadfall as I sat trying to calm my breathing, sure that any moment the doe or the buck still downwind of me would snort and ruin any opportunity for a shot at this bruiser. Eventually, he shifted around until he was almost broadside. I leaned a little to the right in my stand, and found an opening the size of a soccer ball through the limbs of the deadfall, in line with the buck's vitals. I came to full draw, put the sight pin tight behind his right front shoulder, and touched the trigger on my release aid. Elation! The arrow whacked him solidly, the fletching disappearing in the sweet spot to be replaced by a blossom of bright red. I leaned forward in the stand to watch the big buck race away downhill from me. He disappeared momentarily into a ravine, then reappeared running up the opposite slope. He went ten feet or so up the hill, stopped, and slowly tipped over backwards.

It was one of the most exciting and rewarding deer hunts I have ever experienced, and as I climbed down from stand, recovered my arrow, and started down the hill for a closer look at my prize, I couldn't help but reflect on the fact that for a total elapsed time of nearly forty minutes, two does and a buck had milled around downwind of my stand, at ranges varying from 15 to 80 yards, and not one of them had picked up my scent.

Prior to heading out to my stand, I had showered with scent-free soap and shampoo, then sprayed myself all over with a scent eliminator before toweling off. After getting out of the truck, a few hundred yards from my stand, I opened up my sealed plastic bags and put on Scent-Lock undergarments, my hunting clothes, and rubber boots. Finally, I sprayed myself again with a scent eliminator, before making my way to my stand, a 15-foot ladder stand I was able to slip into quietly and with little effort.

Was this regimen the reason I had remained undetected by three deer milling around all that time directly downwind of me? I can't prove it, of course, and I don't pretend that the experience provides evidence that would prove acceptable to a trained scientist. Still, for a hunter accustomed to being busted by most deer that get downwind, it doesn't take many experiences like that one to make getting as scent-free as possible a regular part of pre-hunt preparations.

The entire issue of scent reduction can be frustratingly complex, with various experts reaching different conclusions and one study conflicting with another. It's refreshing to discover a point on which virtually every observer can agree, and here it is: When a deer detects the smell of a predator, or a human, or anything it perceives as a threat, in close proximity, it will waste little time getting out of the area.

Here's another: its nose is the primary defense mechanism of the white-tailed deer.

"Seeing," as the saying goes, "is believing." Which is another way of saying that we humans tend to confirm visually what our other senses tell us. We may think we hear something, and we may think we know what we heard, but we prefer to see it to be sure. In the case of deer, smelling is believing. That is not to suggest that they won't bolt upon seeing or hearing a hunter, but their instinct when they suspect danger is to confirm it by circling downwind and getting a good whiff.

I once rattled in a massive Ohio non-typical buck that raced in from nowhere and put on the breaks not five feet from me. It was a windy day in late October, and I had opted to still hunt and scout as opposed to swaying around in

When rattling, make sure you have complete camouflage from head to toe. If you rattle in a deer and you are hunting alone, he is going to zero in on you and your movement. If you are camouflaged well, and the wind is in your face, a little movement won't be that alarming. After all, he is expecting to see some movement from the bucks he thinks are making all that ruckus. CREDIT TED ROSE.

my stand. In an area where tracks, scrapes, and rubs seemed clustered in an area of an acre or less, I slipped into an opening in a cedar tree, leaned my bow against a limb, and began some high-volume rattling. I hadn't been at it thirty seconds when the buck raced in, put on the brakes, and froze. We stared at one another, eyeball to eyeball, not five feet apart, for perhaps ten seconds. I didn't bat an eyelash, and was dressed head-to-toe in camo, including a face mask. Slowly the buck straightened up, then began circling around me. I knew what he was doing, but couldn't move. Sure enough, as soon as he got downwind he snorted and bolted. Even from five feet away, he trusted his nose more than his eyes.

Small wonder, then, that hunters work so hard to defeat the nose of the white-tailed deer. Many experts suspect that it is impossible to entirely eliminate scent or reduce scent to an undetectable level. Others say that is not the issue, and the reasoning goes something like this: if I am sitting at my computer writing (as I obviously am), and I detect a faint whiff of smoke, I will probably register it on some level, but not react with immediate alarm. If I'm thoroughly engrossed in my work, I may not be fully conscious of the smell, but even if I am odds are I'll finish the sentence I'm writing before investigating. A very strong smell of smoke, on the other hand, will produce an immediate reaction, possibly even close to panic.

Most deer hunters have observed deer that are browsing and relaxed, then suddenly appear to become more alert. The head comes up, and the deer begins looking around. The body becomes visibly tense. The deer may even jump, or run a few feet, then stop. It's not unreasonable to assume, as most hunters do, that the deer has picked up some scent, but at such a faint level that the deer is unable to find the source, or to determine its distance. Were the scent stronger, the deer would bolt, assuming it didn't detect the scent at a much greater distance and avoid the area altogether.

Don't doubt, by the way, that animals with a powerful sense of smell can locate the source of an odor precisely by means of the scent alone. Bird dogs do it routinely. Over the years I've had dogs point quail that were in trees. They didn't look at the ground under the tree, but up into the tree where the bird was not visible. I once had a Brittany point a chukar perched on the roof of a barn. The Brit was momentarily confused, but soon raised its head to look almost straight up at the bird. Deer do learn to look up for danger, but I have to wonder if in some cases it is not so much a matter of an educated deer looking up to spot the hunter, as simply its nose telling it precisely where to look.

Anecdotal and unscientific as these observations may be, the accumulation of them by thousands (millions?) of hunters over the years would seem to be evidence that it is possible, if not to entirely eliminate scent, to reduce it to a level that can make the difference between success and failure in the deer woods.

Assuming this, the real issue for deer hunters might be, to what lengths should we go to reduce our scent. Elsewhere in this book I mentioned that I know of at least two serious deer hunters who shave their underarms during the deer season. I know even more deer hunters who are very careful about what they eat for at least a day or two prior to a hunt. They avoid things like onions, garlic, and in some cases even red meat, which they believe makes them smell like a predator. More than a few deer hunters take zinc during the hunting season, which has a tendency to reduce body odor.

The measures a hunter will take to reduce scent are of course a matter of personal preferences, but here is a regimen followed by most–though not all–of

To help make a decoy more lifelike, add some scent to it. This will further entice a wary buck to get closer to the new opponent. CREDIT TED ROSE.

the more serious and successful deer hunters I have occasion to hunt with. First, they wash their clothes in scent-free detergents, and line-dry them outdoors or in a dryer with a little baking soda. They store them in scent-free containers. Before hunting they shower using scent-free soaps and shampoos, and they brush their teeth and gargle to kill as much bacteria as possible. Most of them do not put on their hunting clothes–at least their over garments–until they arrive at their hunting location. En route to a hunt, they try to avoid being exposed to cigarette smoke, or strong odors such as frying bacon. They wear rubber boots, which also have been stored in a scent-free container. They periodically apply a scent-reducer of some sort, giving special attention to their hats and their boots. Some of them wear scent-reducing clothing that features carbon, or anti-bacterial material such as silver. Some also make it a point to wear rubber gloves when handling decoys, attractant scents and wicks, or when climbing into their tree stand.

Can thousands of successful hunters be wrong? Absolutely. Still, when thousands of experienced, successful hunters with countless years of experience practice such a regimen, it deserves to be given serious consideration. ■

DEFEATING THE
WHITETAIL'S EYES

D efeating a deer's nose is somewhere between difficult and impossible. Defeating a deer's eyes is less challenging. Deer are far from blind, though, and the hunter who underestimates deer vision is going to be seen by deer again and again. Few hunters have never been spotted by a wary old buck or a smart doe as the hunters crossed a field or other opening, made their way down a logging road, or for that matter still hunted through a hardwood forest. The hunter whose tree stand has him silhouetted, or simply leaves him exposed with inadequate cover, is likely to be spotted as well.

A number of strategies can help the hunter evade the eyes of a deer, but before we look at some of these, let's take a close look at exactly how deer see and what their optical capabilities are.

Generally speaking, vision occurs when light enters the eye and is absorbed by various specialized cells at the back of the eye. These cells transmit signals to the brain, which interprets the signals as sight. Color is a function of the wavelength of light reflected from the objects we see. The entire spectrum of wavelengths includes ultraviolet at the short end, and infrared at the long end. Humans and other primates are rare among mammals in that they have very sophisticated color vision, and can see the entire wavelength with the exception of the extremes at both ends. We cannot normally see either infrared light or ultraviolet light.

Deer instinctively stick to cover and shadows. Hunters should too.

PHYSIOLOGY

Physiologically, a deer's eyes differ from a human's in several important respects. At the back of the eyes of all mammals are two kinds of light sensitive cells, rods and cones. Rods function in very low light and allow some degree of night vision. Cones operate in brighter light and allow daytime vision and the perception of color. Humans eyes have three types of cones, which are sensitive to short wavelengths (blue), middle wavelengths (green), and long wavelength light (red).

Deer have more rods than humans, but fewer cones. This suggests they have better night vision, but poorer daytime vision. The specific cones they lack are those that perceive the longer (red) wavelengths of light. Both their physiology and behavioral studies suggest that deer can see shades of blue and green, but not red, and like some color-blind humans, they probably cannot distinguish between green and red.

Deer have larger pupils than humans, to admit more light, further improving their vision in low light. In addition, deer possess a reflective layer at the back of their eyes called a tapetum. (The tapetum is what shines so brightly in the headlights of a vehicle.) This reflective membrane further increases the light available to the deer, again improving night vision.

Another important distinction is that humans have a filter which blocks almost all ultraviolet (UV) light. This permits us to see fine detail better than deer, but limits our ability to see the ultraviolet spectrum of light. Deer lack that filter, which means two things: first, they can probably see better in the UV spectrum, and second, they do not perceive small details well.

What does all this mean, in general terms, for the hunter? To begin with, it means hunters needn't hesitate to wear blaze orange. Where legal, the blaze orange camo patterns are probably effective.

A lot of attention has been given in recent years to the UV issue, specifically the fact that most modern detergents have UV brighteners in them, to make clothes appear whiter and brighter. The concern is that hunting garments that have been washed in detergents with UV brighteners will be highly visible to deer. An entire industry has sprung up providing hunters with special, non-UV detergents, or detergents developed to remove any UV residues from clothing that have been exposed to it. While I'm not aware of any independent studies proving that deer readily distinguish garments washed in UV detergents, their ability to see that portion of the color spectrum suggests that in low light, they probably can see such garments better. Using the stuff certainly can't hurt, and might very well make a difference.

All the data available about how deer see is useful, but like all scientific information, it leaves some questions unanswered and even leads to more questions. Here is one that I have long pondered: if deer have superior low-light vision, why is it I have on so many occasions been able to approach very closely to grazing deer when heading to my stand or leaving it in low light? Apart from remaining downwind of them and pausing whenever they raised their heads, I took no particular efforts to conceal myself, and have often managed to walk to within 20 or 30 yards of deer, usually when they were feeding in groups. Even more mysteriously, this seems to happen not in the darkest situations, but on those occasions when I'm late getting to my stand, before sunrise

Peter Fiduccia, host of the Woods N' Water TV show, with a trophy buck taken at Cree Nation Outfitters in Saskatchewan, Canada. Peter agrees that even though deer see better than humans during the light at dawn and dusk, they are much easier to approach or still-hunt during these times, too. CREDIT FIDUCCIA ENTERPRISES.

but after first light, or when I've left a stand early in the evening, after sunset but well before hard dark. I've even had deer approach me in such low-light situations, seemingly out of curiosity. On one occasion I arrowed a big Kentucky doe that approached me in a meadow at dusk. She appeared to spot me from nearly 100 yards out. When I knelt and nocked an arrow, she sneaked in, stopping several times to bob her head and paw the ground, but eventually approaching to within 40 yards and offering me the shot.

Never have I walked up on feeding deer like this in broad daylight. I've discussed this phenomenon with many deer hunters including, most recently, well-known whitetail expert (and my publisher) Peter Fiduccia. Peter, along with many other experienced hunters, has made the same observation.

Despite this puzzling behavior, the tendency of pressured deer to become almost exclusively nocturnal, together with their ability to run full speed through thickets on the darkest night, indicates that, as the physiology of their eyes suggests, they see very well indeed at night.

How well do they see in the light of day? I suspect they see better than many hunters give them credit for. Turkey hunters like to say that a deer sees a man in the woods and think he's a stump, while turkeys see a stump in the woods and think it's a man. There is some truth in that old saw, but I suspect it has more to do with the tendency of deer to rely more on their keen sense of smell than on any inability to see well. Uneducated or unalert deer will probably not see a motionless hunter standing against a tree or behind a sapling. Once alert, deer are quick to detect even the slightest movement, and will probably spot the human silhouette, or the unconcealed face or hands of a hunter. And as any experienced deer hunter knows, they learn to look up for hunters in tree stands.

Just how good their eyes are is difficult to know, but a lesson I learned in one of my first deer seasons many years ago suggests to me that when they choose to use their eyes, they can see quite well.

I had discovered a clover patch in a hilltop pasture far from any roads. This was marginal farm country, and with a lack of corn, soybeans, or other crops that tend to disperse deer in heavily farmed areas, this four-acre clover patch was a major draw. It was a rare morning or evening when slipping up the logging road and peeking over the hill didn't reveal at least several deer grazing on the clover.

Just into the clover patch, and slightly to one side from where the logging road entered the field, was a big stack of hay bales. The day before the season opener I rearranged them slightly to form the perfect blind, about eight feet up.

Next morning, brimming with confidence, I slipped up the logging road before first light, climbed carefully into my blind, and nocked an arrow. My timing was perfect, or so I thought. I didn't have to wait long before the light was adequate for shooting. I sat expectantly in the hay, peering anxiously through small patches of fog, certain that any moment they would be there. I fantasized about the big eight-pointer I had seen in the area several times, but having yet to tag a deer with my bow, I was ready to take the first deer that offered a shot.

And there it was–across the clover patch, peering out from a thicket, only about 35 yards out, but well beyond my self-imposed limit of 25 yards. It was a small doe, staring intently in my direction. A moment later and there was another, and then a third. My heart pounded as I waited for them to step into the clover and begin feeding. They would only have to get 10 yards from the edge to be in range. Eventually, a large doe stepped carefully into the clover and moved hesitantly in my direction. The two others followed. For some reason, all three were staring intently in my direction. They stopped a few yards from the edge, and the larger one began stamping her hoof repeatedly. I was certain they couldn't see me, motionless as I was in the hay. And novice though I was, I knew enough to set up on the downwind side of the clover. No way could they get my scent.

After a minute that seemed like ten, the old doe turned and bolted, followed by the youngsters. Strange. I couldn't figure it out. I repeated variations on that same scenario several times before I realized what any experienced deer hunter has already figured out: I was pushing the feeding deer out of that clover patch when I moved into my spot. Alerted, they re-entered the clover very cautiously, and though they couldn't catch my scent, they were looking for me, at the very spot where they had heard me enter the clover. And hay or no hay, movement or no movement, they managed to spot me.

More pressured or mature deer would probably not even have entered the clover from that side of the field, but would have circled it carefully at some distance to approach from downwind. And a more experienced hunter would have considered this spot an afternoon/evening stand, not a morning stand. The point, though, is that when deer are alert and using their eyes, they can see quite well.

Aside from the fact that deer, once alerted, will use their eyes very effectively, my experience with those deer in the clover patch points toward one important way to avoid being detected, visually or otherwise, by deer: don't over hunt the same spot. Perhaps more to the point, don't continue to hunt a spot from which deer have picked you off. A deer that has been been spooked in a given location will be extra wary for some time when approaching that location. They will learn to avoid certain spots. Further, as we have seen, there is some evidence that deer communicate alarm with their interdigital glands, leaving scent on the

Using RTVs and other all-terrain vehicles to drop off and pick up hunters, helps keep human scent to a minimum. CREDIT FIDUCCIA ENTERPRISES.

ground that other deer immediately recognize as a danger signal, putting them on alert.

One of the more efficient and effective game/hunting operations I've been fortunate to hunt with is at Enon Plantation, a well-known bow-only hunting plantation in Alabama. The fact that it is bow-only is incidental; any deer-hunting operation could benefit from similar practices. Hunters at Enon routinely see numerous deer on each morning and afternoon hunt. What's more, the deer tend to venture into food plots during daylight hours on a regular basis, and usually seem to be relaxed.

At the opposite extreme, I've hunted at operations in which plenty of tracks and other sign indicated the presence of deer in good numbers, but they're rarely seen venturing into food plots during the day, and when they do they are extremely wary.

How does Enon do it? Two ways, from what I observed. The first is numerous tree stands over a large area. No one stand gets hunted frequently. Further, because of the wide choice of stands available, there is never a temptation to hunt any stand for which the wind direction is not right.

Second, Enon controls how stands are hunted. Hunters are driven directly to their stands, which they can access by taking only a few steps. They are asked to remain in their stand until a vehicle returns to pick them up, and only then should they leave the stand. Because of this approach, any deer that are in or close to the food plot (and there are usually at least a few), run off at the approach of the truck. They never see the hunter enter or climb down from the stand.

Even when a hunter sticks a deer, the folks at Enon suggest he remain in his stand, awaiting the arrival of the vehicle before taking up the trail. These precautions mean that not only are hunters rarely seen entering or leaving their stand, they don't contaminate the area with scent. If the guides at Enon suspect a stand has been compromised–if a hunter reports deer looking up and spotting him, for instance–they either relocate that stand or give it a long rest. The result is that deer at Enon travel more during daylight hours, and tend to be relaxed most of the time.

MOTION DETECTORS

We've seen that deer lack good color vision. The placement of their eyes on either side of their head gives them a very wide field of view, but it decreases their depth perception. They make up for these disadvantages by being motion detectors. As every bowhunter knows, one of the chief challenges of bowhunting is drawing the bow without being seen. Nearly every bowhunter has a story or two about the big buck that was in range but picked up the movement and bolted when the hunter started to draw his bow.

Bowhunters learn to wait before drawing until a deer's head is hidden behind a tree or brush, or at least until its attention is focused elsewhere.

Camo helps, but movement is what whitetail's spot first. Good luck getting to full draw in a setup like this.

Drawing a bow carefully and at the right time aside, there are several ways hunters can minimize the problem of having their movements spotted. The obvious one is overlooked by more than a few hunters: don't move. In a society that values productivity over just about everything else, standing still, sitting motionless, or even walking very slowly, can be a near impossibility for many modern hunters. Hunting situations may at times require moving fast, but the hunter who cannot remain nearly motionless for long periods is at a real disadvantage, and probably spooks game he never knows is there.

There are two keys to remaining still. The first is comfort. The hunter who is not comfortable will have to rely on a tremendous amount of discipline to remain motionless, and eventually all the discipline in the world won't be enough. Hunters who struggle with this should find out what it takes to make them comfortable in the woods, and do it. It starts with the right clothes, but doesn't end there. Comfort might mean a foot rest or a shooting rail in a tree stand. In a blind, it might mean a large blind with a comfortable folding chair instead of a bucket or stool. Nothing is less comfortable than sitting hunched over and cramped up in a blind that is too small and lacks a good seat. On the ground, comfort might require a seat cushion of the kind familiar to turkey hunters.

The second key–which is impossible without the first–is to relax. The hunter who cannot relax in the woods, forget about time, and become totally absorbed in what he is doing, is missing out on one of the best reasons to go hunting, not to mention the fact that he will be a less effective hunter. Deer live always in the here and now, and never look at a clock. Call it New Age Nonsense, refer to it as Mysticism, or even label it baloney if you wish, but you will be a better hunter if you can forget about the workaday world and get in synch with the rhythms of nature. You'll be more alert, and you'll more often make the right decisions at critical moments.

Some hunters achieve relaxation with a routine. For instance, one hunter I know exits his vehicle, walks 100 yards or so into the woods, and stops, sitting or standing, for at least ten minutes. He finds that by simply forcing himself to slow down and take his time, he relaxes. If he is late getting to his stand, or has only a limited time to hunt, he is convinced that it's even more important for him to follow this routine. Hunting in a relaxed, alert state of mind is more important to his enjoyment and his success than saving a few minutes getting to his stand.

Deep breathing is a time-honored method for achieving relaxation. Don't scoff if you haven't tried it. By simply forcing themselves to stop wherever they are and concentrate on breathing deeply and slowly for a couple of minutes, most people find they are able to relax in all but the most stressful situations.

CAMOUFLAGE

It's a rare hunter these days who ventures into the deer woods without camouflage clothing. Even our guns, bows, and gear are camouflaged. Now and then someone makes the observation that as recently as a generation ago hunters, including the most successful ones, ventured afield without camo clothing. That is only partly true. While they may not have worn the kinds of patterns that are popular with hunters today, they tended to avoid light-colored clothing, preferring darker colors, often green or brown. Red was a commonly seen color, too, often in plaid. The old-timers understood that deer did not seem to distinguish red, and felt that plaid tended to break up a hunter's outline. I also recall, from my earliest childhood hunts with my father, being admonished to wear gloves and to keep the bill of my hat low over my brow to shade my face.

Camo can matter. Notice how well these two hunters blend into their background—
and how much their uncovered faces do not.

At the same time, our fathers' generation also didn't hunt from tree stands, and rarely if ever used the kind of fully enclosed ground blinds available to hunters today. Few experienced modern hunters would deny that tree stands or ground blinds offer significant advantages in most deer hunting situations. Wearing colors that game cannot distinguish, along with patterns that break up a hunter's shape and help him blend into his surroundings is camouflage, whether or not the pattern is copyrighted or its name trademarked.

One well-known outdoor writer of my acquaintance, who also acts as a guide on frequent occasions, enjoys hunting without camo. He wears dark clothes and takes other measures to avoid being spotted by game. He gets an extra kick out of tagging animals and ribbing his hunting buddies who are dressed head-to-toe in the latest camo patterns.

The real question, though, is not whether it is possible to tag a trophy buck while not wearing modern camo patterns. It most certainly is. The question is, does wearing camo clothing, and using camo gear, give the hunter an extra edge, if not in every situation at least in some of them? While I would not hesitate to go deer hunting without camo if there were no camo available to me, I'm also inclined to seek every edge I can get, especially when bowhunting. It's just too darned hard to get within bow range of a trophy whitetail to do otherwise.

Breaking up a hunter's outline and wearing dark, non-shiny clothes is important, but if I could camouflage only one part of me, it would be my face. Second choice would be my hands.

On a hunt with a friend in Tennessee several years ago I paused before entering the woods to put some camo paint on my face and hands when I noticed my friend grinning at me. I had to laugh, because I knew exactly what he was grinning about.

"I guess you don't need any of this," I said.

"No, I don't think I do," he said.

My friend, if you haven't guessed, is black. Apparently he found it amusing to watch a hunter pull what looked like a makeup kit from his day pack, flip it open to the mirror in the lid, and start applying camo paint to his face.

The fact is, though, unless you have a very dark complexion, you need to cover your face and hands with camo paint or a head net of some sort. A hunter can be wearing camo head to toe, but if his skin is white and his face and hands are not camouflaged, they will shine through the woods like a full moon on a cloudless night.

Since there are no limits on how much camo I can wear, I generally wear it head to toe. Does the pattern matter? In many situations, probably not. I will wear any pattern as opposed to none, but if I spent a great deal of time hunting sage country in the West, I'd wear a pattern that blended better with the lighter colors of that area, probably one designed to imitate sage. If I hunted primarily in spruce forests, I'd wear a pine pattern. The fact is, I do 80 percent of my hunting in mixed hardwood forests, and have found patterns such as the popular Mossy Oak and Realtree patterns to be effective in environments ranging from southern swamps, to northern forests, to wide-open prairies.

Camouflaging gear is probably less important, the exception being blinds or anything that shines or is highly reflective. The obvious issue is gun barrels and receivers, which tend to be highly reflective if not done in a matte finish.

Remaining undetected by game animals is far more than a matter of wearing camo, climbing trees, or hunting from blinds. (Later we'll look more closely at hunting from tree stands as well as ground blinds.) Whether avoiding the eyes of the hunter's quarry is instinctive or learned behavior could be the subject of a good debate, but a surprising number of hunters take little care to remain unseen.

A few years ago a book high on the bestseller list was entitled *Everything I Need to Know I Learned in Kindergarten*. I cannot quite say that I learned everything I need to know about hunting in kindergarten, but that is about the age at which my education as a hunter began. My father took me along with him hunting in the woods of southwestern Ohio and southeastern Indiana, and the first lessons I learned on those outings were all about how to remain unseen by game animals. I can almost hear my father's voice when I think of them:

"When you come to a field or an open area in the woods, don't walk through the middle of it. Skirt around it. If you have to walk through it, don't waste time; get through it quickly."

"Stay in the shadows and out of the sunlight as much as possible. Walk in the shadows when you can, and when you stop to look around or take a break, stay in the shade."

"Be careful about brushing against saplings and small trees when you walk, and avoid holding on to them when climbing up or down a hill. An animal will hear and see that sapling shake for a long ways through the woods."

"Avoid walking down ridgelines or standing out on points, where you will be easily seen for long distances."

"Avoid walking on game trails or down logging roads when possible.

Animals use these, and you're more likely to be spotted."

"You can often get away with slow movements, but rarely with quick ones. When you look around, turn your head slowly. If you must scratch or get something out of your pocket, do it slowly."

"When you stop, whether temporarily to look around, or for longer periods, stop behind cover that will hide you, but is not too thick to prevent shooting. At least keep cover behind you, to help break up your outline."

"Use the terrain as much as possible–gulleys, hills, creek bottoms, even large rocks or downed trees–to move without being seen."

"Keep in mind the time of day, the time of year, and the weather, to avoid spooking animals. Don't walk through a likely feeding area or bedding area at a time when you might expect game to be there."

"A man standing upright can be seen for a long ways. Stay low when approaching game–hunker down at a distance, drop to your knees as you get closer, and crawl if you need to get very close."

To the experienced hunter, these behaviors are automatic, and require no thinking. And yes, I can imagine numerous hunting situations that represent exceptions–times when shaking a sapling, moving quickly, or even walking through an open meadow–might be the right thing to do. They're good general rules, though, and most hunters would be better hunters for following them whenever there is not a good reason not to.

CONCEALMENT

Thousands of years ago, or so I like to think, one of our early ancestors got tired of chasing game, hid near a waterhole, and discovered a whole new and more effective way to hunt. The lesson was never lost. Deer drives can be a productive and exciting way to hunt, as can still hunting, but it is no secret that the overwhelming majority of white-tailed deer are taken by hunters at a stand of some sort. More than a few hunters simply sit or lean against a tree at a likely spot and wait for game to pass by. These days, even more hunters strike from tree stands. An increasing number use ground blinds.

Whatever the form of the stand, there are steps hunters can and should take to provide as much concealment as possible. We have looked at the advantages of camouflage, and camouflage is important for the hunter who chooses to simply sit or stand by a tree in the woods. Others steps these hunters should take include using breaking up their outlines by remaining in front of some sort

The combination of a tree stand and blind might be the ultimate in concealment.

of dark background in the form of large trees, rocks, or other cover. In addition, hunters can get behind similar types of cover, and can alter the environment to their advantage simply by snipping off small branches and sticking them in the ground at strategic locations. At some point, of course, we're talking about building a blind, but short of that a few small strategically placed limbs can provide significant concealment without blocking off shooting lanes. Deer hunters who hunt using this approach would do well to steal a page from the turkey hunter's handbook, and always carry with them a pair of good pruning shears.

CONCEALING TREE STANDS

It's surprising how many hunters spend hours scouting and picking the perfect location for a tree stand, but give little consideration to keeping the stand hidden. Make no mistake, deer will spot hunters in tree stands. In fact, they do it all the time. Sometimes the easiest way to understand how to do a thing is to look first at how not to do it. Let's take a look at the worst possible tree stand set-up.

It's ten feet high, on the side of a medium-sized tree with no limbs until

Don't forget to make sure the ladder and the stand itself are camouflaged. This do-it-yourself stand was spray painted with black, brown, grey, and green paint. CREDIT FIDUCCIA ENTERPRISES.

about 25 feet up. It's on the side of a hill, facing uphill, with a well-used trail straight ahead, and a cluster of scrapes off to the right, which in this location is to the south.

Problem one with this stand is that it is not high enough. I say this as someone who is not all that comfortable with heights. Height matters. Sorry to all those out there who insist that eight, or ten, or twelve feet is high enough, but it's not. Ask yourself this: If height does not matter, why are we climbing up into trees anyway? Actually there are several reasons, but the main one is to get above the normal line of vision of deer. Deer can and will learn to look up into trees, but it is not something they routinely do. By getting above their normal line of sight, we can more often remain unseen by deer. It's that simple. How high is high enough? I'm not aware of any scientific studies on the subject, and I am open to considering other opinions, but my own experience suggests that at somewhere around 20 feet, a white-tailed deer becomes significantly less likely to spot a hunter. Experimenting with deer I did not intend to shoot, I have literally waved my arms and remained unseen by deer when I was hunting from that height or higher. And yes, I have been spotted at that height and higher, and yes, I have taken deer from stands as low as eight feet. Over the years, though, I have been spotted far more often at heights of 15 feet and less. And I have never gotten away with waving my arms at a deer from 15 feet or less.

Some hunters would argue that 15 feet is an adequate height, and a few of the best deer hunters I know would suggest that the magic number is closer to 25 or even 30 feet. But I do believe this: the hunter at less than 15 feet is better off on the ground. On the ground, he can use terrain and cover to his advantage. Perching 10 or 12 feet up in a tree simply makes him more visible to his quarry, unless he is fully enclosed in a blind.

Though our focus here is on visibility, many hunters also believe that when they are at greater heights, deer are less likely to catch their scent. The theory, which does not seem unreasonable, is that in some situations the hunter's scent will be carried over the head of deer approaching close to the stand.

A related problem with our hypothetical tree stand is its location on the side of a hill. In hill country it's not always possible to avoid such a location, but the hunter does need to keep in mind that even if he is 20 feet up a tree, deer on the uphill side will at some point be at eye level. That may be unavoidable, but a hunter can see to it that a trail, logging road, scrape, or rub line is not at eye level, to decrease the likelihood of deer walking by the stand at that level.

Fully enclosed blinds with darkened interiors, such as the one above, make hunters virtually invisible.

A stand facing east is not necessarily a problem, but the hunter should be aware that if he plans to hunt this stand in the morning he may, depending on the steepness of the hill, find himself looking directly into the sun. Morning stands facing the rising sun to the east, or evening stands facing the setting sun to the west, can leave the hunter nearly blinded for a good while on clear days, and can be downright uncomfortable.

Hunters are often advised to position stands in such a way that deer are more likely to be looking into the sun, but I have some doubts about the soundness of that advice. First, the primary consideration far and away is wind direction, and the likelihood seems low that the perfect set-up with regard to wind, among other factors, will position hunters so that deer are likely to be looking into the sun to see the stand. What's more, if the sun is behind the hunter, he is likely to be casting a long shadow. If concealment behind the hunter has him completely shaded, this is not a problem. But if so much as the top of the head or one arm is at any time touched by sunlight, the hunter's slightest movement will be exaggerated by a giant shadow on the ground. It's far better if no portion of a hunter's shadow extends into the area where he expects to see deer.

Finally, our hypothetical tree has no limbs until the 25-foot mark. That is just the kind of tree many of us look for when using climbing stands, but it leaves us hanging out there in the great wide open, where deer–especially mature deer–are almost sure to spot us. Drawing a bow without the movement being picked up can be all but impossible in a stand of this sort, but rifle hunters will often get spotted here as well. In this kind of stand, even the absolutely motionless hunter can and probably will be seen by deer.

There are fixes for that problem, including various blinds designed to conceal hunters in tree stands. Trimming limbs and properly positioning them around the stand with wire or nails can help address the problem, in areas where hunters have permission from landowners to do this. There are also artificial limbs on the market that can be used in these situations to help provide concealment. Also among products that can be useful here are umbrellas such as Eastman Outfitters' Sta-Dry Umbrella. From the perspective of a deer looking up, these provide a background to which hunters can blend in, and simply keeping hunters shaded makes them less visible also. Decoys can be useful here, too, by helping to keep the attention of an approaching deer on the decoys and away from the hunter, though decoys in themselves are no substitute for some degree of concealment.

Many hunters turn an otherwise excellent stand into something less than that by over pruning. Some judgment is called for here. It's an exercise in frustration to sit in a stand with inadequate shooting lanes that would require a deer to stop and position itself in one of two or three spots for the hunter to have a good shooting opportunity. At the same time, over pruning can call attention to the hunter and leave him exposed. There is a happy medium between adequate concealment and adequate shooting lanes, and only good judgment and experience will tell the hunter when that point has been reached.

EYE CONTACT

Is eye contact is an issue in concealment? Though some hunters might scoff at the idea, most veteran hunters have reached the conclusion that many prey species, including deer, understand that when eye contact is made, they have been spotted. More than a few hunters have stopped to scan a nearby deadfall or thicket, only to have an animal hidden there bolt the moment eye contact is made. Among many species of animals, staring is recognized as a threat, and animals, including most canine species , will show submissive behavior to a dominant member of their own species by turning their heads and looking away. More often than not among canines, two animals staring at one another is the first step toward more overtly aggressive behavior which usually leads to a fight. It doesn't seem at all out of the question that prey species should evolve in such as way as to recognize through eye contact when they have been spotted.

Hunters have developed some interesting approaches to this problem. One, of course, is to avoid staring (at least when the quarry is close) by not looking directly at the animal, looking instead to one side. Eventually, it's

An uncovered face will shine through the woods like a full moon on a cloudless night. Covering the face and hands is probably more important than wearing a specific pattern.

difficult for a hunter to avoid looking at what is about to become a target. My friend Chip Hart, with whom I co-host *The Big Outdoors* radio program in Cincinnati, swears by sunglasses, developed specifically for the purpose, that allow hunters to see perfectly while completely hiding their eyes with a camo pattern. Many hunters–and I confess to doing this myself on occasion–try to squint in such a way that they can still see, but the whites of their eyes are mostly hidden. It would be difficult to prove that these methods work, but it's hard to imagine they can hurt.

MOTION DETECTORS

We've already mentioned that deer are great motion detectors. The best conceal-ment is unlikely to work if a hunter makes exaggerated movements. It's important that the stand be arranged in such a way that movement can be kept to a minimum. That limb part way around the tree trunk might be suitable for hanging a daypack on, but only if it can be accessed without any gynmnastics. Could be I fidget too much, but I frequently access my day pack for water, snacks, calls, or other items. Bows and rifles, too, should be in easy reach. Holders attached to stands work very well. My own preference when bowhunting is the EZ Hanger, or similar devices that are affixed to the tree over the hunters' head, with the bow hanging immediately in front. With this arrangement a hunter can have bow in hand with only the slightest movement. Still other hangers and organizers of various sorts are available for hanging calls and other accessories, all neatly organized and close at hand. There is nothing worse than frantically digging around in a daypack for an item that has become suddenly very necessary.

One of the more interesting approaches to reduce the likelihood of being spotted in tree stands involves the use of dummies. I've seen this trick used most often in tripod stands where concealment options are limited, but it can be used in any tree stand. A simple, home-made dummy of some sort, usually con-sisting of an old jacked stuffed with pillows or straw, with an improvised head wearing a hat, is left in the stand at all times when it is not occupied. The idea, of course, is that any deer spotting the stand will become accustomed to the general shape of a hunter in it, and will not react to the real thing. I can't speak to this from personal experience, never having tried it. It makes sense, though, assuming deer don't pick up a hunter's scent.

GROUND BLINDS

The first hunter probably used ground blinds of some sort. Even four-footed predators will remain hidden behind deadfalls, thickets, or trees, waiting to pounce on any prey species that walks by. Humans simply improve on that tactic by in effect creating their own deadfalls, thickets, or trees. They can usually improve considerably on the "blinds" that happen to occur naturally, and enjoy the huge advantage of being able to put them wherever they want them. (That is only an advantage if they know where to put them, but we'll get into that later.)

The corollary to this is that prey species have learned that predators like to use cover for setting up ambushes, and many of them have learned to avoid danger areas, or to pass by them with extra caution. A young goose or turkey might wander close by a big tuft of grass or a row of standing corn, but older ones will usually give them a wide berth, preferring to remain out in the open where they can see all around.

Deer are a little different in that they often prefer thick cover themselves for concealment, relying heavily on their keen sense of smell to avoid danger. Still, mature deer are wary enough to be cautious around anything new or unnatural in their environment. Which suggests two keys to success in using a blind for deer hunting: make sure it's not "new," and try to make it appear as natural as possible. Both things are very doable for the hunter willing to take a little time.

When they work, ground blinds feel almost like cheating. Almost.

Making it not "new" is as simple as setting it up in advance. Even a blind set up in the middle of a wide open pasture is something deer will become accustomed to if they see it repeatedly and decide it's not a threat. How long that process take depends on how often the deer pass by it, and probably a little bit on the individual deer itself and how wary it is. Longer is better, but the hunters I know who are consistently successful from ground blinds prefer to have a blind in place at least several days before hunting from it.

That is not always possible for any of several reasons, and in any case that strategy tends to negate one of the chief advantages of using a ground blind, which is mobility. Many of today's newer blinds, designed to be set up and taken down very quickly, allow hunters to observe the ever-changing travel patterns of deer and take advantage of their observations by setting up a blind from which to ambush them.

Which leads us to the other key to success in using ground blinds; that is, making them appear as natural as possible. I use the term "natural" here, because it is the kind of jargon with which hunters are familiar. On a farm in south central Ohio is an abandoned barn surrounding by thick, second growth penetrated only by a network of well-used game trails. I have used that barn as a blind on several occasions. There is also a rusted out old pick-up truck in the corner of a field close to where a logging road enters the field, and I have spent a few hours sitting in that truck, too. There is nothing natural about either of them, but deer accept them as part of the landscape because they have been there a very long time.

Making a blind appear natural is mostly a matter of breaking up an unnatural silhouette. Cover behind the blind helps, but it can be important to have some cover in front of the blind, as well. In many spots it is possible to set the blind up in such a way that some natural cover is all around it, and that may be sufficient. In other cases, hunters will have to manipulate the habitat a little. A log or limb on the ground in front of the blind can help anchor it and keep it from flapping, as well as break up an unnatural straight line along the ground. Additional concealment can be as simple as leaning a few limbs, real or artificial, against the blind. Many blinds have ties at strategic locations to facilitate this process. By backing off and looking at the blind, it's not hard to tell when the silhouette is less discernible. As with providing concealment for a tree stand, some judgment is in order. The idea is to provide concealment while insuring that adequate shooting lanes are available.

Keeping blinds shaded can be helpful here. Aside from the fact that blinds in direct sunlight can get uncomfortably warm in all but the coldest weather, sunlight will make any unnatural aspects of the blind more visible. Also, some fabrics reflect sunlight, creating a very unnatural shine. When a given environment or location requires setting up a blind in the open, it becomes increasingly important that it remain there for some time before being hunted.

While a fully enclosed blind can go a long way toward concealing a hunter, sharp-eyed game animals can still pick them off if they can see inside the blind. One way to avoid that is to keep the interior of the blind dark, by putting it in the shade. Better still, many newer blinds have black interiors for this purpose. A hunter wearing camo or dark clothing, whose face and hands are covered, will be virtually invisible from outside the blind unless he gets very close to the opening. This is another advantage of comfortably large blinds. It can be impossible to stay back from the opening in a smaller blind, and a smaller blind may even require that arrow or gun barrel extend outside the window. The careful gun hunter can usually get away with this, but it's a real disadvantage for the bowhunter.

There is some concern that shooting windows can be problematic in blinds with black interiors. From outside the blind, these windows when open appear as large black spots, and a lot of anecdotal evidence suggests that deer will shy away from these. In fact, the folks who make Double Bull blinds are convinced that this is the case. They recommend keeping the shoot-through camo mesh netting in place. Hunters inside the blind can see through the netting, but from the outside the netting blends in perfectly with the camo pattern of the blind. I have shot rifles, shotguns, and arrows through this netting without difficulty or any perceived loss of accuracy. There are a couple of limitations on bowhunters using this netting, though. Not all mechanical heads will work with them, since the camo netting will open the heads prematurely. In general, L-shaped or wing-blade mechanicals won't work, while other designs such as the Rocket Steelheads will work. I would highly recommend trying any mechanical heads before shooting them through the netting in a hunting situation. String trackers will not work with the shoot-through netting.

Finally, there is the issue of scent and ground blinds. Some hunters have suggested that ground blinds tend naturally to reduce scent, since they block the wind and may tend to contain some scent inside the blind. A few of the newer blinds actually include the same carbon-impregnated fabrics as Scent-Lok

Pruning to clear shooting lanes is often necessary, but should be done cautiously so as not to leave hunters totally exposed.

suits. At least one blind I'm aware of is sealed and actually vents the hunter's scent through a tube high into the air. These are fairly recent developments, and I can't speak to their effectiveness from personal experience.

INCREASING RANGE

About five years ago, on a plantation hunt in southern Alabama, I sat in my tree stand over a greenfield as dusk approached and watched a forkhorn emerge from the woods across from me and to my left, about 150 yards out. I watched him with curiosity, and then a beautiful if smallish six-pointer walked out behind him. When a third buck in the 130 class emerged behind the six-point buck, I sat up at full attention. In single file the bucks made their way out to the middle of the field, then turned on a path that would take them directly in front of me. Slowly but steadily they made their way down the length of the field as various does here and there looked up from their grazing to watch.

As I brought my bow to full draw, part of me hoped it would be too dark, and that I wouldn't be able to see my sight pins. The bucks were passing by at 50 yards, and that was a good 10 yards beyond my self-imposed limit of 40 yards. I could see my fiber-optic pin sights just fine, though. I put the bottom pin level with the top of the biggest buck's shoulder and tracked as he walked slowly by, tempted sorely to touch the release. As he passed my position, I let down slowly. I felt I probably could have made a good hit on the buck, but "probably" just isn't good enough. I try hard to avoid taking any shot that I don't feel very confident about.

It was frustrating, though. On that same hunt were several friends for whom a 50-yard shot is routine, and they would take any open shot at a broadside whitetail out to 60 yards. I vowed on the spot that I was never again going to watch a Pope & Young whitetail walk by my stand at 50 yards because I couldn't shoot confidently out to that range.

I began practicing to increase my effective range the day after I returned from that trip, and have since taken several deer at ranges of 50 yards and slightly beyond. I discovered that increasing effective shooting range can not only enable a hunter to take shots at deer that would not otherwise come into range, but the ability to make longer shots can also make a hunter less likely to be detected, whether through sight, sound, or hearing. To the firearms hunter, this is probably a small factor. To the bowhunter, though, this can be a significant factor.

There is an irony here: one of the reasons many hunters take up bowhunting,

Extending maximum range through practice with bow or gun is one way to defeat the eyes, ears, and nose of a white-tailed deer.

and one of the things they enjoy most about this form of hunting, is that it is up close and personal. For the bowhunter, the thrill of waiting motionless as that big buck moves slowly into bow range is unmatched by any other hunting experience. Nonetheless, part of the challenge of hunting, whether with firearm or bow, is shooting accurately at extended ranges. The bowhunter who has the time and the desire to practice regularly can extend his range to 50 or 60 yards. Some bowhunters can shoot with confidence at deer-sized game at even longer distances. Ethical hunters do not take shots unless they are confident of a good hit, but for those willing to put in the practice, there is no denying that the ability to shoot game at 50 yards, as opposed to 25, decreases the likelihood of being picked off by wary bucks, and increases the likelihood of shot opportunities. ■

It takes plenty of range time to be able to shoot at distances longer than 150 yards. It also requires confidence in your firearm and using the right ammunition for shooting at longer distances. This range, made of old barn beams, provides many hours of shooting practice for its owners. CREDIT FIDUCCIA ENTERPRISES.

DEFEATING THE
WHITETAIL'S EARS

or whatever reason, the subject of how deer hear has drawn less scientific attention than how deer smell or how they see. Most of the research that has been done has been done with the aim of producing devices to prevent car-deer collisions. The focus of those studies has involved primarily the frequency ranges to which deer respond, and the short answer to the question is that their hearing is very similar to that of humans in terms of the frequencies they hear, with some biologists suggesting they can hear slightly higher frequencies.

For the hunter, it may be sufficient to know that white-tailed deer hear sounds at slightly greater distances than do humans, and that they seem better equipped to pinpoint sounds both in distance and in specific location.

As hunters, we do have this going for us: the woods are usually full of sounds. Birds chirp, squirrels bark, chipmunks whistle, sticks pop, leaves rustle, limbs squeak, and the wind sighs through the trees. And, at least in the places where most of us do most of our hunting, vehicles pass by, planes fly over, dogs bark, roosters crow, chain saws rumble–as often as not, it's downright noisy out there. At a certain level of noise–on a windy day, for instance–deer feel vulnerable and tend to bed down. Short of that level, they will move normally. They will react to the constant sounds around them in much the same way as will a hunter. They will tune out the bird song or the leaves rustling in a breeze. They will be startled by any sudden loud noise that is close by. Unlike human hunters they are not at the top of the food chain, so they will almost certainly run from it. They will register other sounds that are not overly loud or do not originate from very close by, becoming more alert and waiting to determine the source with their sense of smell, or visually. They might even assume the sound was made by another deer.

Deer (and other animals) can certainly learn to distinguish humans moving through the woods from other critters simply by sound, but only because careless humans make sounds that differ from those of any other creature. Only humans consistently crash through the underbrush, and only humans walk with a constant, regular cadence. Hunters who refrain from making either of these sounds by picking their path more carefully, by varying their pace, and by stopping frequently to look and listen, can often avoid being "made" by alert deer. It is possible to walk quietly through the woods, stepping softly and avoiding the sticks and rocks that betray our location.

Finally, I am amazed by the number of hunters who talk in the woods. The human voice is very distinctive, and carries over great distances. To some extent remaining unheard in the woods is, like remaining unseen in the woods, a matter of instinct or early training. For those who have the instinct or the early training, there is a natural tendency to remain quiet in the woods.

RIG FOR SILENT RUNNING

Years ago I was among the last handful of young men to be drafted into the U.S. army. The war in Vietnam was winding down rapidly, and I was fortunate enough to serve my time here in the states. I didn't know that would be the case when I was in training, though, and I have a very vivid memory of one particular training exercise at Fort Knox. My platoon, in full field gear, made its way on a ten-mile hike through the woods by moonlight. Boots stomped the ground, steel helmets clanked, canteens gurgled, loose ammunition rattled, and hardly a minute passed without someone feeling an irrepressible urge to cough, sneeze, or say something to the man in front of him or the guy behind him. I made a mental note to myself to look for a desk job or try to get into the sniper program, because I didn't think my chances for survival in combat would be very good if my buddies were as noisy as this bunch. In retrospect, I have to assume that more advanced training was in store for anyone headed for a combat zone.

Hunters are not normally in life or death situations, of course, but they do have a need to be quiet. In part, that means learning how to move quietly through the woods. It also means having the right gear and using it correctly, beginning with the right clothing. The standard for comparison is wool. Wool has several advantages to recommend it, including its ability to shed moisture and retain some insulating ability when wet, but wool is also typically a very quiet fabric. That means not only that it doesn't swish when the wearer walks, but that it doesn't make loud scraping or zipping sounds when a stick, thorn, or other object rubs against it. Fleece is another relatively quiet fabric, which is one reason for its popularity with hunters. Cotton, depending on the weave, can be quiet, and can be a good choice for mild weather hunting.

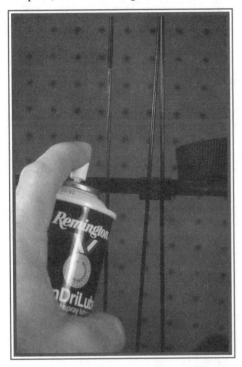

Details matter. Dry lubes such as Teflon can quiet squeaky cable guard slides.

Until a few years ago, rain gear was unavoidably noisy. Newer blends of waterproof breathable fabric, especially when combined with fleece or wool, can be very quiet. Whatever the style garment, testing for quiet is easy enough. If it doesn't swish or make excessive noise when rubbed together, and if it doesn't scrape loudly when a thumbnail is rubbed over it, it's probably acceptable for hunting. Just keep in mind that on a quiet day in the woods, even the slightest rustle of clothing can cause a deer walking under a tree stand to bolt.

Buttons make for the most quiet closures. Zippers, if they don't have to be accessed too often, might do. Velcro is noisy.

Clothing aside, the hunter who heads into the woods without making some preparations with silence in mind is probably going to sound a little like my platoon at Fort Knox. Fanny packs and daypacks are great items, but unless packed properly loose items will rattle in them, liquids will gurgle, and metallic buttons will clack. Combine these with a tree stand, a bow, or a rifle, and the noise intensifies. Quieting these items doesn't require a course in engineering—just the time to assemble everything, walk around with it for a minute, and take the necessary steps to ensure that it can be worn or carried together quietly.

Most hunters have a story or two about the big buck that almost was, and in many cases the difference between a tagged deer and another "one that got away" story comes down to a tiny detail. On a filmed muzzleloader hunt in Missouri a few years ago, a cameraman and I were crossing a drainage in a cut-over cornfield when we spotted a good buck less than 100 yards away and dropped to our seats in the mud. The drainage was overgrown with saplings and high grass, and the buck was walking along the edge of it on a path that would take him right past us. I scooted to a deadfall that would offer a little more cover as the cameraman hastily set up his tripod and got in position.

After what seemed forever but was probably about two minutes, I could

Small, long-distance two-way radios are great tools when hunting. Their use should be limited, though (check the state laws where you are hunting regarding radio use). Advise the group leader you have arrived to your stand and when you are going to leave. Other times you should use your radio are when you have downed an animal and need some help to get it out or for a medical emergency. They should not be used for idle chitchat. CREDIT FIDUCCIA ENTERPRISES.

see the buck's legs through the thick second growth. I got glimpses of him several times, but couldn't get an open shot, and then he stepped into the open less than 20 yards away, walking with his nose to the ground. Working to control my breathing, I pushed off the safety of my muzzleloader and was surprised to see the buck suddenly turn and bolt out of sight behind the cover. I had no idea what had spooked him, but the cameraman knew, because I was wearing a mike and he had on a headset. He easily heard the click of the safety going off, and clearly, so did the buck. It dropped, turned, and ran at the sound.

The sound of a sling swivel clacking against a rifle barrel, the sound of an arrow being drawn over a noisy rest, the sound of a jacket sleeve swishing as an arm is raised—all these sounds and many others have saved more than a few deer from winding up on a plate or on the wall. The hunter who pays attention to those details will still probably lose a deer or two to unpredictable noises. The hunter who doesn't will surely spook many deer, some of which he will never know were there.

We made reference earlier to the fact that carrying tree stands through the woods can compound the difficulty of moving quietly. The need to silence tree stands, though, doesn't end when it comes off the back. Even worse than rattling through the woods en route to the stand location is rattling, squeaking, or creaking when in position on the tree, with game approaching. Tree stands seem somehow to get better every year, and the days of metal scraping metal and chains rattling with every movement are fortunately over for the most part. Still, it's worthwhile applying a little oil (or better still, grease) to any moving parts of the stand before hanging it. Some hunters customize their stands, and quiet them further by applying carpeting, which has the added benefit of comfort and warmth.

HEARING AND HUNTING TACTICS

Should the whitetail's hearing ability be a factor in hunting strategies? Absolutely. I occasionally enjoy still hunting, for instance, but on those crisp, dry fall days when hardwood forests are carpeted with leaves, still hunting is not the best option. Even moving at a snail's pace—which is generally the proper pace for still hunting—the hunter is going to make noise that will alert deer, possibly for hundreds of yards. On the other hand, deer have the same problem. The hunter on a stand can often hear deer approaching from great distances under such conditions. Getting to and from the stand without creating a

Veteran deer hunter Peter Fiduccia regularly rakes leaves off the trail to his tree stands. He says that not only do you get to your stand quietly, but the deer also wind up using the trails too!
CREDIT FIDUCCIA ENTERPRISES.

commotion is difficult. Hunters can sometimes wade along the edges of lakes or ponds, or use creeks or creek bottoms, to avoiding wading through dry leaves, and this is a situation in which walking along the edge of an open field, or even crossing the middle of one, can be the best approach. If the stand is not far from a creek or a field edge, hunters can sometimes even keep a path open to the stand to approach it in complete silence.

When the woods are damp, or when a steady breeze maintains a constant level of noise, is a great time for still hunting. Such conditions are also great for hunting standing corn. Deer often bed in standing corn, and when a light breeze tends to cover movement and sounds, the careful hunter can sometimes slip up on deer in their beds. The technique is simple, which is not to say easy. The wind must be coming from a direction that enables the hunter to move across (as opposed to down) rows while simultaneously moving more or less into the wind. The hunter steps very carefully and slowly from one row to the next. At each row, he leans his head forward slowly into the next row, looking up and down the row. When the field is crossed, the hunter can retrace his steps quickly downwind, move over thirty or forty yards (depending on visibility in the corn field) and start again, eventually in this way working through the entire field.

A pair of compact binoculars can be helpful. Seldom will the hunter see

Always carry binoculars in your backpack. Even though you may be posted in a dense area where the best shot is a close one, you never know what you may see far away on your way in or out from your stand. CREDIT TED ROSE.

an entire deer, or even a large portion of it. More often he will spot a patch of brown or white fur, or catch the flick of an ear or tail. It's often impossible to be sure how the deer is oriented, or which part of it is visible. The trick is to move very slowly into position, or wait for the deer to stand or move. Often, a stone or clump of dirt tossed into the air to come down on the other side of the deer will cause it to stand or turn its head. Getting into such a position can take hours or days–then again, getting a shot opportunity from a stand can take hours or days, too. Cornfield stalking is an exciting way to hunt deer, particularly for those hunters who prefer not to sit in a stand.

Walking through a cornfield at a varying pace can trick a buck in to staying bedded longer than normal, giving you an opportunity for a shot. CREDIT FIDUCCIA ENTERPRISES.

DEER DRIVES

Is there a time when a hunter might want to be heard by deer? There is, and I'm not talking about calling or rattling, which are subjects for another chapter. Hunters on a drive might very well want deer to hear them, since the idea is usually to move deer in the direction of other hunters.

The mistake that some hunters on deer drives make is that they think in order to drive deer effectively, they should make as much noise as possible. In most situations that is not the best way to drive deer, for several reasons.

First, counter-intuitive though it might be, a lot of noise doesn't necessarily frighten deer, and can even reassure them. Deer, as with most prey animals, seem to instinctively understand predatory behavior when they see it. If two men walk down a logging road at a brisk, steady pace, talking as they go, the reaction of a deer bedded close to the road will probably be to lie motionless and let them walk by. The deer hears them coming for some distance, so he is not startled by them. At the same time, he does not perceive them as a threat. He knows exactly where they are at all times, and their behavior does not suggest that they are hunting.

Contrast that with one or more men slipping along quietly and slowly. They vary their pace, occasionally stopping and looking around. It is possible that they will get close to a deer before he detects them–close enough that the deer will be startled by their sudden appearance and bolt. And even if the deer is not startled, it will immediately recognize the behavior of such men as a possible threat. Most experienced hunters have at one time or another stopped and stood in one spot for a minute or two, for any of a number of reasons, only to suddenly have a rabbit dash off through a thicket, or a covey of quail explode from the cover of a deadfall. Had they continued walking steadily, they'd never have seen the rabbit or the quail, but when they stopped the critters got nervous and fled.

Works with deer, too. On a deer drive, moving slowly and quietly can not only increase the opportunity that a driver will get a shooting opportunity (assuming safety permits), but will probably move more deer past hunters on stand as well.

BODY LANGUAGE AND HEARING

In his book *Whitetail Strategies*, Peter Fiduccia devotes an entire chapter to interpreting deer body language. It's interesting and useful stuff, and I'd like to reference a portion of it that is relevant to the subject of this chapter.

If you're watching a doe and both ears are forward, Peter points out, the doe is probably alone. However, if one ear rotates toward the back, she is probably listening for deer that are following her. It could be a pair of yearlings or another doe, but of course it could be a buck, too.

Those large, cupped ears help deer pinpoint the location of sounds, and they will often rotate them toward the source of a faint or distant sound. Keeping an eye on those ears, and watching for something to approach from the direction they are pointed, only makes sense.

Bowhunters tend naturally to worry more about sound, because they must get relatively close to deer. Most of them have at one time or another made a sound that spooked a deer they were preparing to loose an arrow at.

I would suggest, though, that gun hunters should pay equal attention to the noise they make. Bowhunters know they are spooking deer, because the deer are close and react to the sound. Gun hunters, some of whom are less careful about noise, are probably spooking some deer without ever knowing they were there.

STRING JUMPING

So you're in the right spot at the right moment, the planets are properly aligned, the wind direction is right, the hunting gods are smiling, and a thousand-and-one things finally come together to put a trophy buck standing broadside 25 yards from your stand with you at full draw and the sight pin settled tight behind his shoulder. You touch off the release and watch in amazement as the buck turns and runs. There was no satisfying "whack," and the buck showed no signs of a hit. You climb down from your stand and find your arrow, which confirms what you already suspected: a clean miss. But how? The shot felt so right.

Until we began studying slow-motion video footage, jumping the string was something only a few bowhunters suspected was possible. Now we know it's not only possible, it happens too often. As an outdoor writer, I occasionally have the opportunity to participate in the making of hunting videos or television programs. As you might imagine, any time a hunter being filmed has a close encounter with a whitetail, the evening's entertainment invariably includes sitting around replaying the footage. We congratulate the successful hunter and commiserate with those who miss or have other mishaps. On several such occasions I've watched slow-motion footage as arrows sailed over the backs of bucks that successfully jumped the string. The dejected hunter nearly always sits up in amazement. He thought he had simply made a bad shot; now he knows he made a good shot, the buck just dodged the arrow. Still, a miss is a miss, whatever the reason.

How the term "jumping the string" originated I can't imagine. "Ducking the string" would be a better description of what happens. At the sound of the release, the startled deer drops and simultaneously turns. I think it unlikely the deer is knowingly dodging the arrow. He's simply crouching in preparation to spring away at a dead run. The effect, though, is the same as if he were intentionally dodging that arrow. The arrow flies over the back of the target. While I've not yet had a deer successfully jump the string on me (not one that I can be sure wasn't just a clean miss, anyway), I have taken several deer with liver shots that I suspect were the result of the arrow catching the deer as it dropped and turned. The aim was for a low lung shot, the result was a hit that was a little high and a little far back.

ANATOMY OF STRING JUMPING

Before we look at what we can do to reduce the occurrence of string jumping, let's look at the anatomy of a string jumping incident–how and when it usually happens, along with the various factors that will give us some indication of what can be done about it.

Many writers contend that it is impossible to entirely prevent a deer from jumping the string, and the reasoning goes something like this: the speed of sound is over 1,100 feet per second. A very fast arrow travels at around 300 feet per second. Therefore, the sound will always reach the deer before the arrow, making it impossible to eliminate string jumping. That is well and good, but it leaves out one very important variable, which is the reaction time of the deer. Granted, deer are extremely quick. They are not instantaneous, though. They do have a reaction time, and it must be factored into any such equation.

If the potential reaction time of a white-tailed deer has even been calculated, I am unable to find such information. This is another of those instances in which we will probably have to settle for anecdotal information. And the anecdotal information I have collected over recent years suggest to me that, all else being equal, deer are significantly less likely to successfully jump the string when the arrow is moving at a very high speed. Numerous experienced bowhunters have expressed to me the opinion that as arrow speeds have increased over the last decade or so, the incidence of string jumping seems to them to have decreased.

The bugaboo here is "all else being equal." All else is seldom equal. Some bows are naturally more quiet than are other bows. Further, super fast bows are likely to be louder than slower bows. That is changing, though. Bow makers are getting very good at silencing bows these days, and some very fast bows shoot more quietly than some older but slower bows.

Another factor involved here is distance to target. The farther away the target, the faster the sound reaches it relative to the arrow. A deer at 30 yards has more time in which to react than a deer at 15 yards. I didn't pick these numbers randomly, though. At 30 yards or more, deer seldom jump the string, and the reason is that the sound is not so loud or threatening at that distance. A sound that would startle a deer at 15 yards often has little or no effect at 30 yards. At the same time, a very fast arrow reaches the deer so quickly at a range of 15 yards or less that string jumping is rarely an issue at these ranges. The critical distance for string jumping–that is the, the distance at which it seems most likely to occur–seems to be in the 18 to 28 yard range, with occurrences falling off rapidly at ranges under or over these.

HOW CAN WE PREVENT STRING JUMPING?

What does all this suggest, in practical terms? The best thing most hunters can do to reduce the likelihood of string jumping is to make their bows as quiet as possible. That means, among other things, using string silencers. String silencers are inexpensive, so it's worthwhile to experiment and try different types. Positioning makes a difference, too. Slide the silencers up and down the

string short distances. It's difficult to shoot and listen, so have a friend stand nearby and listen for the differences. There are other string damping devices on the market, such as Saunders' Deadly Quiet, which attach to cable rods and stop the string from twanging after the shot while actually boosting speed a little.

Some bowhunters put moleskin or other types of padding in limb pockets; this might be helpful, if done carefully, on some older bows,

String silencers are great for reducing noise. Have a friend stand nearby to help you detect the best position.

but more current models usually won't benefit from this, since bow manufacturers are building sound dampening materials into modern bows.

Stabilizers can help quiet bows, as well as reduce torque and enhance balance, and most bows can benefit from a stabilizer. In addition, limb dampening devices such as Sims' LimbSavers or NAP's Thunderblox significantly decrease vibration and sound.

Accessories are another matter. Sights, rests, quivers, peeps–virtually anything that can attach to a bow–are potential sources of clacking, buzzing, and rattling. As with bows, manufacturers are doing a better job all the time of quieting these items. Many now include sound dampening devices, to the extent that some quivers are even billed as doing double duty, quieting bows in addition to holding arrows. I still like to insert moleskin padding between my accessories and contact points with the riser of the bow.

We mentioned that speed itself can decrease the incidence of string jumping, and that is true. The only caveat I would add here is that given a choice between quiet and speed, go for quiet. Further, all the speed in the world does not compensate for overdrawing a bow and the subsequent deterioration in accuracy, along with the increased likelihood of arm or shoulder problems, that overdrawing brings.

At least one very successful bowhunter I know insists that he always aims low, directly under the deer, because the deer is going to try to jump the string every time. It's hard to argue with success, but I am certain that if I aimed under every deer I shot at, I would shoot under quite a few. Like many bowhunters, though, I do tend to aim for low lung shots. It only seems reasonable to give oneself a little latitude if possible. As I mentioned earlier, I have taken a few deer with liver shots that I suspect were the result of deer attempting to jump the string. Aiming a little low might have made the difference in those cases. Further, a low hit increases the likelihood of a good blood trail.

Bows and accessories aren't the only source of unwanted noise. Often the culprit is arrows. And as arrows become increasingly lighter, noise becomes a bigger problem. Heavier arrows are always lighter than light arrows, again assuming all else is equal. (Which it never is.) Contact problems with the rest can make noise, in addition to robbing accuracy. Often the problem is as simple as loose inserts or broadheads. Use Lok-Tite or similar products to keep screw-in broadheads on tight.

Finally, fletching makes noise. I happen to prefer feathers, but there is no denying they are noisier in flight than are vanes. If you stand safely downrange, off to one side behind a solid object, you can hear feather fletching as it buzzes by. Are deer more likely to jump the string when a bowhunter is using feather fletching? Based on my experiences I would have to say no, but there are certainly hunters whose opinions I respect who are convinced that deer are more likely to jump the string when feather fletching is used instead of vanes.

Finally, bowhunters are sometimes advised to shoot only at relaxed, unalert deer.

If you would watch a huge buck walk by your stand in range because it appeared to be alert, wary, or anxious, my hat is off to you. Most of us, I suspect, are going to take the shot if we can get it. Naturally it is better to shoot at relaxed deer when possible. If a deer is feeding and raises its head, even if I'm already at full draw, I'll be inclined to wait a few seconds for it to lower its head again. Usually, though, we are waiting for any kind of reasonably open shot we can get at a deer that is stopped or walking slowly in range. When the shot presents itself, take it. More than a few trophy bucks have escaped hunters who passed up a good shot because they were waiting for a perfect shot. Knowing the difference is a matter of skill and experience, but beginning hunters would be well advised to learn the difference as soon as possible. ■

HOW SMART ARE DEER?

We've looked at the whitetail's phenomenal olfactory capabilities, along with its keen sense of hearing and its vision, which provides it with a wide field of view and a well-developed ability to detect motion. Perception, though, is meaningless without an ability to make sense of all the input and react intelligently.

Just how smart are white-tailed deer? Several factors complicate any exploration of that subject, beginning with the fact that every hunter wants to think his quarry is a challenging and worthy adversary, and part of being challenging and worthy is being smart. Hunters thus have a built in bias. Even more complicating is the tendency to attribute human characteristics to animals. In the Introduction, I mentioned that when I was a kid, I was told by some old-timers that smart old bucks would send does and fawns ahead of them through the woods, so the bucks would be at less risk. That is something humans might do, but in the case of deer a much more likely explanation—and one for which some strong evidence can be cited—suggests that before and during the rut, bucks often follow does. Another classic example might be the fisherman who suggests that a certain fish hit a certain bait or lure not because it was hungry, but out of anger or frustration. Maybe so, but we really have no way of knowing if a fish experiences anger or frustration, let alone being able to determine with any degree of certainty which of several possible motives it responded to in a given situation. People once thought birds sang because they were happy; now most of us understand that singing is usually a way for male birds to declare their territory, or to attract mates. Many people believe a dog wags its tail because it is happy: some biologists suggest a dog wags its tail as a sign of submission to a superior, while other biologists believe tail wagging is simply a means of dissipating excess energy. My children tell me that my brittany knows its name, but I'm doubtful. I don't believe that dogs know what a "name" is. I suspect my dog has learned that when it hears the sound "Chester," it is about to get some sort of attention, or is about to hear some other sound, such as "Hunt 'em up!" or "Stay!" or "Fetch!" which it wants to respond to, or has learned it had better respond to.

In any case, that tendency to attribute human emotions or reasoning processes to animals is what scientists refer to as anthropomorphism. Nothing like science to take the fun out of things, and many people would much prefer to think that birds sing and dogs wag their tales because they are happy. That is fine—it might even be correct—but anthropomorphism has its downside, not the least of which is that for many people, the next step beyond attributing human emotions and reasoning ability to animals is giving animals moral equivalency to humans, or even moral superiority. For deer hunters, another downside is the possibility that we will develop hunting strategies based on misunderstandings of behavior.

Finally, another complication is that "intelligence" is a somewhat vague and relative term, and is notoriously difficult to measure. Are deer as smart as dogs? Are they as smart as pigs? Wild turkeys illustrate the problem here very well. Many turkey hunters—and I am an avid turkey hunter myself—will tell you that turkeys are very smart indeed. They say this because they find turkey hunting challenging, and because on so many occasions they have been defeated by them in one way or another.

On the other hand, wild turkeys are completely baffled by a woven wire fence, and if they have never encountered one (or in some cases, even if they have), they can be observed to walk into the fence, bounce off it, and walk into it again repeatedly. Eventually they will fly over it or walk around it, but it seems to take some time to figure that strategy out. This behavior does not suggest a high degree of intelligence.

Turkeys are challenging to hunt, I would suggest, not because they are intelligent, but because they are extremely wary, have excellent vision, possess amazingly quick reactions, and lack curiosity—that is, they tend not to wait for confirmation of anything suspicious in their environment, but to avoid it if it's at a distance, and run or fly from it if it's close. (On the other hand, the fact that turkeys are capable of some learning is suggested by the fact that they are far less challenging to hunt in areas where turkey hunting pressure is light, and correspondingly much harder to hunt in areas where they are regularly hunted.)

That deer and other animals are capable of learning there can be no doubt. Exactly what and how much they can learn may always be subjects of debate. A thorough discussion of animal psychology is beyond the scope of this book, not to mention the expertise of this writer. Still, a basic understanding of how most animals learn (and how they don't learn) can be helpful in forming judgments about how deer are likely to respond to a given situation or hunting strategy.

Some behaviors are simple reflexes, hard-wired into an animal's physiology. Most animals will be startled by a sudden loud noise, for instance, and will jump or run in response. Other behaviors are instinctive. In some cases instinct is clearly at work, while in others it can be difficult to distinguish entirely between what is instinctive and what is learned. For instance, when a robin builds a nest, this appears to be entirely instinctive behavior. The care that a doe gives her fawn may appear to be instinctive, but deer that are raised in isolation from all other deer may not care properly for offspring, and does that have had offspring in the past are likely to provide better care than those giving birth for the first time. Both these phenomena would suggest that caring for young is at least partially a matter of learning, as opposed to purely instinctive.

Other behaviors are more clearly a matter of learning. A deer that has never encountered a certain food–corn, for instance–will probably not respond immediately to the sight or smell of corn. Eventually, after some exposure, deer will sample the corn and learn that it is indeed a desirable food.

Behavioral psychologists speak in terms of various sorts of conditioning, but a common factor with regard to how most animals learn is association. Essentially, through experience they associate one thing or event with another thing or event. The association may be positive or negative, but it has little to do with any sort of logic or abstract reasoning.

As an example, when I was in my teens I bought a beagle pup. The pup had never been outside the kennel in which it was born, with the exception of twice-daily romps around a fenced in yard. I made the mistake of putting it on the floor of my car in the backseat, and the bigger mistake of bringing with me an uncle who smoked cigars. Not surprisingly, the pup got sick on the ride home.

After that, it got sick every time I put it in the car. In fact, simply putting the dog on a leash and leading it toward a car made the pup drool, foam at the mouth, and begin vomiting. The moment the dog believed it was about to be put into a car, it was sick. It associated cars with illness.

Curing my beagle was a long and difficult process that involved first allowing the pup to become comfortable in the bed of a motionless pick-up truck, and rewarding it with a treat. Eventually, it wanted to get in the bed of the pick-up truck. Over time, I drove the truck slowly with the dog in it, gradually increasing the length of each trip. Soon I was able to entice the dog into an automobile to get a treat. There were some setbacks along the way, but over time the dog learned to associate automobile rides not with being sick, but with getting a treat. When it later learned to associate getting into a vehicle with going hunting, it was all I could do to keep the dog out of vehicles.

Humans can form such associations, too. They are often the basis for phobias of various kinds, or other irrational fears. However, our ability to use logic and abstract reasoning enables most of us to understand when such an association is irrational, and as a result we can usually get over it. One of my children, for instance, gets sick when she reads in the car. She understands that it is reading that makes her ill, and refrains from reading in the car. If she weren't capable of that kind of understanding, she might very well associate illness with the car and, like my beagle, become ill any time she thought she was about to get into a car.

What does all this have to do with deer hunting? A lot, I think.

Will a deer react negatively to the smell of cigarette smoke? It is possible that deer have an instinctively aversive reaction to any sort of smoke. I've never observed them running amuck when a farmer burns trash in his yard, though. And some deer attractant scents are made in the form of smoke, which carries curiosity or food scents downwind to attract deer. I suspect that how a deer reacts to cigarette smoke depends on whether or not the deer has learned to associate the smell of cigarette smoke with humans. No doubt many have in areas where deer occasionally come in contact with humans. In remote areas where contact with humans is rare, such an association would be unlikely. To take this a step further, imagine deer that come into such frequent contact with (non-hunting) humans that they have no fear of them. In that case, they may associate cigarette smoke with humans, but not with danger, because they don't fear humans.

How will a deer react to the scent of apples? Quite possibly a deer will not react to the scent of apples at all if it has never encountered an apple.

Assuming, though, that deer in an area are familiar with apples, many hunters suggest that it would be a mistake to use apple scent (or any other attractant scent) in a location where there are no apple trees, or where the deer has never known apples to be present. Perhaps so, but that would require a level of fairly abstract reasoning that I am doubtful deer possess. I simply do not believe that a deer in that situation will stop to wonder if it is strange to be smelling apples in an area where there are no apple trees. (Actually, I doubt that a deer has any concept of "strange" at all.) The deer simply smells apples. If he is hungry and wants apples, and if that desire takes priority over the alfalfa field he is headed for, or the doe he is following, or any number of other factors that influence his behavior, then he will come in to eat apples.

If a bruiser buck winds you from your stand, do you return to hunt it the next day?
CREDIT TED ROSE.

Similarly, is it a mistake to use estrous doe scent weeks before any does in the area are likely to come into heat? Probably so, but not because a buck detecting the scent will consult a calendar and decide that something is wrong. It's a mistake because it's a waste of time–testosterone levels have probably not yet reached the point at which a buck is likely to respond to a doe in heat.

Here is another scenario: you're bowhunting, and Mr. Big walks by your stand, 30 yards out. You overestimate the range and put an arrow just over his back, at which point, predictably enough, he runs off. Do you abandon that stand?

Some experts may disagree, but I say no. The buck has no idea what that arrow is, or where it came from. He may have been startled or experienced a momentary sense of danger, but he felt no pain and nothing gave chase. It seems unlikely that, based on that isolated experience, the buck will avoid the area.

On the other hand, if a buck's behavior suggests that he smells or sees a hunter in the stand, it may very well be time to abandon that stand, at least temporarily. The deciding factor is, did the buck or did it not associate that particular spot with danger?

A representative for Bio-Logic feeds once said to me, "I hope we never really figure deer out. It will take the fun out of hunting them."

He's right, of course. Fortunately, I don't think we're all that close to totally figuring deer out. I suspect there will always be room for debate about the kinds of issues we've looked at in this chapter. In any case, an inquiring mind, a healthy dose of skepticism, and a continuing interest in how (and how much) deer learn can enhance a hunter's enjoyment of deer hunting while giving him an edge other hunters won't achieve. ■

HOW ONE MAN TURNS THE TABLES ON WHITETAILS

A s an outdoor writer, I've had the opportunity to get to know a number of well-known and truly expert deer hunters. All of them have some characteristics in common, but no two of them agree on every aspect of deer hunting, and each has developed his own approach to deer hunting.

My friend Johnny Webber is not so well known as some other deer hunters, largely because Johnny doesn't make a living writing about deer hunting, or making hunting videos, or marketing hunting products. Every deer Johnny has killed has been taken within 40 miles of his southeastern Indiana home–and he has taken more trophy bucks than all but a few of the best nationally known deer hunters, who regularly hunt the hottest spots in the U.S., Canada, and Mexico. I want to discuss his approach to deer hunting here not as the best or the only way to take trophy whitetails, but simply as the way that one very dedicated, experienced, and successful deer hunter approaches the art and the science of deer hunting. Some of his techniques are by the book, and some are in defiance of it. That is because, while Webber reads a great deal about whitetailed deer, his approach to hunting them is based largely on his own observations and experiences over a lifetime of hunting.

Let's start with what he does that is more or less by the book. To begin with, he scouts like a man obsessed–which he is. He scouts year-round. He scouts when he drives to work or to the grocery, or just about anywhere else. He is always looking for deer and places to hunt them. I suspect he scouts when

Webber with just a few of his southeastern Indiana whitetails.

he's at the dentist's office or the barber shop, too, because he knows nearly every serious deer hunter in three counties and talks deer hunting whenever he runs into a deer hunter. That's not to say he doesn't scout by putting his feet on the ground; he does plenty of that, too. Especially in late summer, he spends a fair amount of time glassing fields at dusk, when the big bucks often come out in the open. When he hunts a place, he knows it. He knows where the deer are bedding, where they're feeding, and how they get from one area to another. He knows big bucks are in the area, or he wouldn't be hunting there.

Actually, Webber doesn't hunt an "area." He hunts spots.

"I don't normally hunt a stand because good bucks are in the area and a certain stand looks like it's in a good spot," Webber once told me. "I hunt a stand

Webber scouts open fields from a distance in late summer to learn the whereabouts of big bucks.

because I have reason to believe that a good buck walks by that stand fairly often."

Webber does not rattle for bucks, believing that the buck-to-doe ratio is too skewed in southeastern Indiana to make that a good tactic. For the same reason, he does not hunt over scrape or rub lines.

He does occasionally use a grunt call. He also occasionally uses doe urine. He washes in unscented soap, and often applies raccoon urine to his boots.

This book focuses on how deer use their senses to evade hunters. Here is why I say Webber turns the tables on whitetails: whitetails make use of their superior senses to elude hunters. Webber relies on his senses–mostly his eyes

Being able to identify certain deer from the tracks they leave is a skill highly regarded and fine-tuned by many successful hunters. CREDIT FIDUCCIA ENTERPRISES.

and ears–and on his knowledge of whitetail habits, to pursue them aggressively until he catches up with them. With the exception of those hunters in the more northerly latitudes who are skillful at filling tags by tracking deer in the snow, I know of no deer hunter who so effectively takes the game to the whitetails, playing cat and mouse with a buck until he eventually succeeds in hunting him down.

Webber hunts whenever he has the opportunity, but is a great believer in putting days together whenever possible, as opposed to hunting sporadically over time. Feeding patterns, travel routes, and general behavior change through the fall and winter, and Webber is adept at staying on top of these changes. He believes, though, that hunting sporadically a day here and a day there is a handicap, and that by putting hunting days together for at least three days in a row, and preferably five or six or more, he greatly improves his chances of figuring out the buck he wants and filling a tag.

He is a persistent, but not a patient, hunter. Discipline enables him to sit in a stand from first light to last light on occasion, but the moment he loses confidence in a given stand, he abandons it and moves elsewhere.

Several years ago he phoned me to tell me about a 150 class buck he had just taken.

"Two different guys hunted a stand about 200 yards from where I got this buck," Webber told me. "After I got this buck, both of them told me that in the last few days they had seen him and another buck going up the drainage where

I got him. One of them saw the bucks twice, so that's three different times they saw these bucks in the course of a few days. But you know what they did? They stayed in that stand. Instead of climbing down and going over and putting a stand in that drainage where they were seeing the bucks move, they stayed where they were. I put a stand up over there and filled my tag right away."

That is the essence–if somewhat simplified–of how Webber hunts whitetails. He closes in on them. By seeing them, hearing them, or finding their sign in the form of fresh scrapes, rubs, or tracks, he figures out where they are going and when, then finds a spot along the route from which to ambush them. It's a game of cat and mouse in which he may move his stand again and again before getting a shooting opportunity.

It helps that he excels at reading sign. He's an excellent tracker, and can usually identify individual deer by their tracks. For the trophy hunter, it is one thing to see that deer are regularly and recently moving along a ridgeline or up a drainage, but it's another thing altogether to see that a specific big buck or two is among them. Johnny is also very good at estimating the size and quality of a buck by examining its rubs. He once told a farmer he was after a big-bodied 10-point buck with one brow tine that was much bigger than the other. When it came out that Webber hadn't yet actually seen the buck, but was convinced of its large size and its uneven brow tines on the basis of having examined several of its rubs, the farmer scoffed. A few weeks later Webber knocked on the door to show the farmer the big 10-pointer that did indeed feature an odd combination of one long and one short brow tine.

I mentioned earlier that Webber employed a few tactics that are not exactly by the book. The first one has to do with height. Webber likes tree stands that are 30 feet or more off the ground. For hunting during Indiana's shotgun or muzzleloader seasons, his attitude, in a nutshell, is the higher the better. He'll stay a little lower for bowhunting, but still prefers to climb higher than most bowhunters want to go.

Why so high? Two reasons. First, he is convinced that the height makes it significantly less likely his presence will be detected by deer. Obviously being up in nose bleed territory puts him well above the line of sight of any deer. He is also convinced that in many cases it carries his scent over their heads.

The second reason is the vantage it gives him. I mentioned earlier that Johnny scouts year round. That doesn't stop when the hunting season starts. He continues scouting during the season, both when he is hunting, and sometimes when he is not. A high vantage point enables him to see deer in the distance that he would not otherwise know were there. Every sighting is another bit of useful information that helps him form a continuously evolving picture of where the deer are going, where they are coming from, and when they are moving. Spotting a big buck in the distance once is a useful piece of the puzzle; spotting a big buck close

To really get to know the deer in your hunting area, scout during the off-season. Take a stand in the morning or evening to see the activity of the deer during this time of year. CREDIT FIDUCCIA ENTERPRISES.

to the same spot twice means Webber is probably about to put up a new stand.

As someone who is uncomfortable at heights much beyond 20 feet, I can't personally follow Webber's lead on this point, nor would I recommend that any hunter climb to heights at which he is uncomfortable. I do believe, though, that climbing to the maximum height at which one feels comfortable and safe does decrease the likelihood of being spotted by deer, and may reduce the likelihood of being scented, as well.

Webber will use climbers, by the way, when he needs quick mobility, but prefers other types of stands whenever possible, believing that climbers usually create too much noise and commotion.

Probably the most unorthodox tactic Webber employs is intentionally jumping big bucks from their beds. It's not something Webber recommends doing early in a season or during the peak of the rut, when bucks are likely to be moving during the day anyway. At the same time, it's not entirely a last-ditch tactic, either. Webber will do it when deer movement is minimal for an extended period, or when he goes for several days running without seeing deer, or when he simply feels that he does not have a good handle on where or when bucks are moving. Here's how it works.

Webber knows, from thorough scouting and his general knowledge of whitetail behavior, where the bucks are likely to be bedding at a given time on a given property. Leaving his bow or his gun at home, and carrying with him only a stand, he'll cover ground, wading through all the areas where he believes good bucks may be bedding. He is not looking for tracks, or rubs, or scrapes. He wants to jump the buck and get a decent enough look at it to be sure of its quality. When he jumps the buck, Webber stops and studies the location. The objective is to determine where the buck enters and leaves its bedding area. He then puts up his stand and leaves the area. He waits three days before hunting from that stand, but when he begins hunting it, he hunts it hard, confident that sooner or later he will catch the buck entering or leaving the area.

Once, on a scouting foray, Webber showed me a huge, deeply gouged rub on a tree with the girth of two telephone poles. It was high up on a hill in a sparsely timbered area, and noticing that it was within sight of a country road that wound along the creek bottom below, he decided to return to the rub and cover it with black paint. I was not surprised that a hunter who works so hard and dedicates so much time to hunting trophy whitetails would want to reduce the likelihood that possible poachers would see a good rub and hunt his favorite area, but I was impressed by his tendency to think outside the box, as well as by the extent to which he will go to give himself every edge in his efforts to tag a trophy buck.

The question arises: would Webber be an even more successful hunter if he adopted such tactics as creating mock scrapes, rattling, or using sex, food, or curiosity scents? Possibly, though he enjoys the kind of success that would be hard to improve upon through any means. What I am sure of is this; most any deer hunter could improve his success rate with the hard work, persistence, knowledge, and willingness to learn and adapt that are the key features of Johnny Webber's approach to hunting white-tailed deer. ■

Johnny Webber likes to get as high as he can to minimize his chance of being spotted by a deer. Use the height of a treestand to your advantage, but stay in a stand that is only as high as you are comfortable with. CREDIT FIDUCCIA ENTERPRISES.

DECOYING DEER

O ne way to defeat a deer's eyes–and even use its vision against it–is to use decoys. There are several reasons to use decoys. The first and most important reason is that they work. They don't always work, any more than any other strategy always works. Like calling, rattling, or most other hunting tools or strategies, decoying deer works just often enough to make it worthwhile. Decoys offer several advantages. First, a decoy can bring deer into range that would otherwise be out of range, and can cause deer to linger in the area. Second, a decoy can distract a deer from the hunter, making discovery less likely and giving the hunter a better opportunity to get off a good shot. Finally, a decoy can help position a deer properly, in a shooting lane, at the best angle. These latter two points are of more importance to bowhunters, but they can certainly be helpful to gun hunters, as well. By causing deer to spend more time in the area, decoys can also provide any hunter with a better opportunity to evaluate the quality of a deer and decide if it is a shooter.

There is another good reason to use decoys. We needn't dwell on this overly long, but using decoys is a lot of fun. Deer do not always see decoys, but when they do, they nearly always react. How they react is unpredictable, which is part of the fun. Often they approach a decoy cautiously, bobbing their heads and pawing the ground. Occasionally they rush in. Sometimes they attack the decoy. Bucks may attempt to mount it. On a few occasions, I have had deer run from a decoy, but in all those cases they stopped, turned, and approached the decoy again. In some cases, deer will remain for quite a while in the vicinity of a decoy, watching it carefully as they browse, occasionally stomping the ground or approaching it, or bobbing their heads in an apparent attempt to make the decoy move.

My most recent successful experience using decoys is one that I recounted earlier in a chapter on scent. Because I was using decoys on that hunt, and because I think it illustrates some of the advantages of using decoys, along with some typical decoying strategies, I'll recount it again briefly, this time with a focus on how the decoys were used. I was hunting at Thunder Valley Outfitters in southern Iowa with my friends Steve Bailey and Steve Lorenzo of Renzo's decoys. It was early November. The weather had been unseasonably warm, with little deer movement, but temperatures dropped nicely the night I arrived, and everyone in camp was optimistic bucks would be cruising or chasing does.

Flight delays and a missed connection meant that I didn't arrive in camp and get to my bunk until around 3:00 A.M. and, exhausted from an entire day of travel, I slept in. I got to my stand a little after noon.

The stand was near a hilltop in rolling, wooded country, though there were crop fields nearby. I made my way to the stand carrying two of Renzo's silhouette decoys, a buck and a doe. At Steve Bailey's suggestion, I put the doe in a bedded position, with the buck behind her. In order for deer to be able to see the bedded doe, I put them in a fairly open area near a logging road. That meant they were over my left shoulder, somewhat behind me, but the stand was positioned in such a way that I could easily turn to make a shot in that direction. I placed a white handkerchief doused with doe urine in a slot made for that purpose on the doe decoy's rump. Bailey is a strong believer in scent-control, and at his insistence I used rubber gloves when handling the decoys. I climbed into my stand and noted that a slight but steady breeze was coming from my left.

I had been in the stand a little over two hours when a doe approached from the left, moving with the wind at her back. She crossed in front of me about 15 yards out, and was almost past me when she spotted the decoys. Immediately she stopped and stared intensely at them. After a minute she sneaked off, directly away from me, for about 70 or 80 yards, then stopped. Again she stared at the dekes for some time, then began approaching them cautiously, stopping now and then to bob her head or stomp the ground. Eventually she wandered off again, but never got more than 80 yards away, seemingly fascinated with the decoys.

About fifteen minutes later, another doe came through from the same direction. She passed by, then stopped and began browsing just downwind of

When hunting with decoys during the rut, don't forget to bring your grunt call along. Using a grunt call will help entice curious bucks into the decoy . . . and into shooting range! CREDIT FIDUCCIA ENTERPRISES.

my stand and about 30 or 40 yards from the dekes in the open area.

But this one had a buck following. It came along a couple of minutes later, and I judged it to be about a 140 class–a definite shooter. It was watching the doe, which may be why it never spotted the decoys. It stopped behind a deadfall not 15 yards away. When the doe it was following moved off a short distance, the buck followed at a fast trot. My grunts were to no avail, and it was moving too fast for a shot when it crossed my shooting lanes. When the doe stopped about 80 yards away, the buck stopped too. I could see the tops of its white tines shining through the woods. Discouraged at having a nice buck pass by so closely without offering a shot, I began trying to lure it back into range by grunting.

After the second or third grunt, I heard an answering grunt, not from the buck I was watching, but from another buck somewhere off to my left. He grunted in response to my every grunt, and then I saw him, walking stiff-legged in my direction. I estimated him to be a 160 class buck, and began struggling to control my breathing. I'll admit I might have been shaking just a little bit, too. I came to full draw as he approached, waiting for him to step into a shooting lane. He didn't oblige. He stopped behind the same big deadfall as the first buck, a little further out at 25 yards or so, but this one saw the decoys. The moment he spotted them, he began grunting more steadily, then putting on a show by thrashing around at several nearby saplings, along with the limbs of the deadfall. When I couldn't hold at full draw any longer, I let down as slowly as I could. Perhaps because his attention was fixed on the decoys, he didn't' spot the movement.

The extra time gave me a chance to calm down a little and get my breathing under control, but I was worried. There were two does and a buck all more or less downwind from me. The doe and buck pair remained where they had stopped about 80 yards away to my right, and the first doe had wandered back toward the decoys and was no more than 30 yards from me, directly downwind. I was convinced that one of them would soon catch my scent and send the whole gang running off through the woods.

The bruiser buck showed no sign of stepping into my shooting lane. Intent on displaying his dominance to the decoys, he continued to punish the saplings around him. He did shift around some, though. I leaned off to my right a little and found an opening the size of a soccer ball through the deadfall. When the buck shifted position a little more, he moved into the opening and offered me

This Iowa bruiser responded to a combination of decoys and calling.

a shot that was almost broadside, quartering toward me slightly. It wasn't the ideal shot for a bow, but convinced that the other deer were going to catch my scent, and confident I could put the arrow through the opening where I wanted it, I came to full draw, put my top sight pin tight behind the buck's shoulder, and touched the release.

I was rewarded with the solid "whack!" that every bowhunter lives to hear. The fletching disappeared in the sweet spot as the big buck kicked, turned, and bolted down the hill. He disappeared down into a ravine, scrambled up the opposite slope about ten feet, stopped, and tipped over backwards. He's not yet back from the taxidermist as I write, but I gross scored him at just under 160.

I'll never know for certain, of course, but I'm convinced the decoys made a difference on that hunt. They did not bring the buck in–he came from a direction that would not have allowed him to see them until he was close–but they did hold him in the area. Without them, I suspect he'd have behaved much as did the first buck.

TYPES OF DECOYS

Essentially, there are two types and two genders of decoys. The genders are obvious enough: bucks and does. The types are full-bodied, or 3D decoys, and silhouette decoys. There are variations on those themes, including some very solid silhouettes that are on the heavy side, and some very lightweight foam decoys that are three dimensional.

We'll look at gender first. If the quarry is a doe for the freezer, the choice is a no- brainer. Does tend to avoid bucks. It is true does may actively seek out bucks when they are in heat, especially in areas where buck-to-doe ratios are close to even, but as a practical matter, the great majority of does already have a suitor or two in hot pursuit as soon as they approach estrous. Does are always more likely to avoid, than to approach, a buck decoy.

As social creatures with a high degree of curiosity and a definite pecking order, does will often approach doe or fawn decoys. I won't pretend to fully understand their motives, but their posture and body language when approaching doe decoys suggest a desire to figure out who this stranger is, along with an inclination to demonstrate dominance in the pecking order, or at least establish which is to be the dominant of the two.

When the quarry is a trophy buck, many hunters are convinced that a buck decoy works better than does a doe decoy. Bucks are naturally inclined to demonstrate dominance toward other bucks. Some buck decoys are smallish in body size as well as rack, to decrease the likelihood that any passing buck will be intimidated by the decoy and shy away from it. Big bucks will sometimes ignore very small ones, though, so the best bet is probably to use a buck decoy that approximates the average buck in the area being hunted.

At the same time, more than one hunter has watched with amusement as a buck attempted to mount a doe decoy. Hunters can add wagging tails (more about this later), and appropriate scents to present the image of a doe that is ready for action. Since bucks and does tend to be segregated most of the year, doe decoys probably are most effective for bucks only during or close to the rut.

If you put out a buck decoy, make sure it has a small set of antlers. This way, all sizes of bucks will come out and won't be intimidated by a "larger buck." CREDIT TED ROSE.

An obvious way around the problem of whether to use doe or buck decoys when buck hunting is to use one or more of each, as I did with the Iowa buck. If a buck is annoyed at the sight of a strange buck in his area, he is (assuming the rut is at or near full swing) likely to be enraged by the sight of a strange buck with a doe.

Choosing between full-bodied and silhouette decoys is largely a matter of personal preference. Each has its advantages and disadvantages.

The full-bodied decoy is exactly that–full bodied and three dimensional, fully visible from any direction. Some hunters believe full-bodied decoys to offer more realistic presentations, but that is debatable. They do offer greater stability in windy conditions. The downside to many of these decoys is that they are relatively heavy and cumbersome to carry. The best decoy in the world will not be effective if a hunter stops using it because he gets tired of lugging it around. This may not be an issue for hunters using ATV's, or hunting stands over food plots or logging roads to which they can drive.

Silhouettes have the obvious advantage of being lighter and easier to carry. They fold up and can be carried on belt hooks in some cases. A related advantage is that hunters can easily take two, three, or more silhouette decoys to their stands, something that is difficult to do with the heavier full-bodied decoys even when hunting the most accessible stands. Strong winds can be problematic for many silhouette-type decoys.

Whether the lack of three-dimensionality is a weakness or a strong point is a debatable issue. Steve Bailey suggests–and I have seen behavior that would confirm it–that putting out several silhouette decoys arouses curiosity in deer, and presents the illusion of movement. A deer circling several properly positioned silhouette decoys will find decoys alternately appearing and disappearing as it circles. Further, in terms of realism, some modern silhouette decoys are essentially life-sized photographs of deer. From a distance, they can be virtually indistinguishable from the real thing.

LOCATING AND POSITIONING DECOYS

Decoys obviously won't work if they are not seen, which suggests using them in more or less open areas. Food plots and meadows are good bets for decoys, as are logging roads or mature, open woods where visibility is good for long distances. I have experienced situations, such as the Iowa hunt previously recounted, in which deer did not see decoys until they were within bow range, but the decoys still proved useful for distracting the attention of deer from me, as well as for keeping the deer in the vicinity until a shot opportunity presented itself. Having said that, it still only makes sense to try to use decoys and position them in such a way as to make them visible for long distances.

There are exceptions, but decoys tend to work best when positioned upwind, which is the direction most hunters are going to be facing in any case. Bowhunters naturally need to keep the decoys in close. Some experts recommend as close as ten yards, but I've found myself handcuffed a few times when using decoys that close, and have come to prefer setting them up at 15 to 20 yards. It's an easy matter to pace off or measure the distance, so the decoys can serve as benchmarks for estimating the range of approaching deer.

To some extent, hunters can influence shot position, and even the route deer will follow getting to the decoys. Bucks tend to approach buck decoys from the front, doe decoys from the rear. Doe decoys tend to approach other doe decoys from the front. The logical positioning of the decoy, then, would usually be broadside to the hunter–assuming the use of one decoy. If several are being used, position can be varied. In fact, if the decoys are silhouettes, it is important

Since bucks tend to approach doe decoys from the rear and does approach doe decoys from the front, it is a good idea to place a doe decoy broadside to your stand. CREDIT FEATHERFLEX.

that positions vary so that deer can see at least one decoy from any direction. By placing decoys strategically near deadfalls or other kinds of cover, it may be possible to further influence the approach taken by deer, but keep in mind that if the cover is too large it will serve mostly to prevent the decoy from being seen from certain directions.

Deer decoys have come a long way. Before commercial decoys were developed, decoys like this were used as far back as the 1960s. CREDIT FIDUCCIA ENTERPRISES.

DECOY TRICKS & TACTICS

Placing decoys in highly visible locations increases the likelihood they will be seen, but does not guarantee it. Further, stiff, motionless decoys are not entirely natural, and may even suggest alarm or aggression to deer. Adding life to decoys, in the form of motion, is one of the easiest and most effective strategies the hunter can use. It will increase the likelihood that your decoys will be spotted and, once they have been spotted, some motion will tend to put deer at ease, increasing their confidence and the probability that they will come in for a closer look at the decoys.

Author, publisher, and Woods N' Water television show host Peter Fiduccia makes another excellent point about the importance of motion in deer decoys. Peter has observed that when deer spot decoys from some distance, they tend to get over any initial nervousness they show, especially when motion is imparted to the decoy. However, if deer moving by a stand suddenly spot decoys from close range, they tend to be startled and often become very nervous—a nervousness that they often don't get over.

Peter began experimenting with decoys many years ago and, being the unorthodox hunter he often is, came up with some very unorthodox—but effective—methods of decoying deer. Some of his early experiments involved putting a shoulder-mount doe on one side of a tree and hanging a stuffed deer rump on the other. This was effective, if clumsy to carry. Noticing that the rump itself seemed effective, he soon eliminated the shoulder mount and began using the rump alone. Eventually, partially because of embarrassment at carrying a deer rump around, and partly out of concerns for safety, he eliminated the hindquarters, too, except for the tail. This he could carry safely and discretely, not to mention easily. And it worked!

Here's the approach Peter came up with: he collects deer tails during the season, cleans and brushes them, secures them between a couple of pieces of cardboard with a rubber band, and sticks them in the freezer. A few weeks prior to the next season, he removes them from the freezer, cuts a hole in them near the top, and airs them out. He hangs the tail about ten or twenty yards from this stand, a little over two feet high. It's important that visibility be sufficient that deer can spot the tail, but not so wide open that the tail is obviously disembodied.

Noted deer hunting authority Peter Fiduccia invented the deer tail strategy in the 1980s and has used it with tremendous success for the past 25 years. CREDIT FIDUCCIA ENTERPRISES.

The key to the success of this simplest of decoys is motion. Peter attaches about 30 yards of string to the tail, with the other end attached to his wrist if he is on the ground, his ankle if he is in a tree stand. The most effective technique seems to be to occasionally wag the tail slowly, and slightly. Fast or exaggerated motions are to be avoided. Peter has found that the tail alone can bring deer into bow range, hold them in the area, and in many cases position them for a shot.

In more recent years, Peter has begun experimenting with the use of full bodied decoys as well. He emphasizes that with these decoys, too, movement is important.

Peter is a great believer in total simulation, sparingly using scent with his decoys when the time is right. He also uses grunts and rattles in combination with decoys. Peter believes its important to avoid calling aggressively when using a decoy. The idea is to get a buck's attention and lure it in, not intimidate it with aggressive tactics.

There are battery operated tail wagers and similar kinds of devices designed to create movement in decoys, and these can be effective where legal. At the other end of the spectrum, a white handkerchief simulates a tail and will move in a breeze. White tissue paper can work even better if properly secured, since even the slightest puff of a breeze will cause it to move.

There is one limitation that we would be remiss not to mention, though, and that is the issue of safety. Many hunters will not use decoys of any kind on

Peter Fiduccia with a buck he shot after it came in to a natural deer tail decoy. CREDIT FIDUCCIA ENTERPRISES.

public land, but even on private land some discretion is in order. The photorealistic silhouette decoys in particular should be used with great caution during gun seasons. Personally, I will not use them if I'm bowhunting during gun season, since bowhunters normally place the decoys close to their stands. Carrying decoys in and out of the woods should be done carefully, with the decoys covered. Some decoys feature blaze orange coloration on the ears or other visible areas–a good idea, since deer can't see it but hunters can.

Assuming safety and local game laws are kept in mind, the only limitation on the use of decoys is the imagination of the hunter using them. They're effective, and they add an exciting and often entertaining element to deer hunting.

CALLING DEER

id you know that behavioral scientists have catalogued at least 147 distinct vocalizations of white-tailed deer, taught them to respond to over 300 human sounds and gestures, and determined that deer in general, and whitetails in particular, possess a surprisingly subtle and sophisticated vocabulary?

Well, they haven't. I made that up. Deer are graceful, wary, amazingly adaptable animals with impressive survival skills. Still, they are animals. They don't "talk." They do make certain sounds, though, that seem to communicate fear, anger, contentment, or a desire for sex or companionship. Biologists or other experts often disagree about exactly how many distinct vocalizations whitetails make, but the number is probably somewhere around a dozen. In addition to vocalizing, deer communicate by stomping their hooves and by thrashing their antlers against trees or saplings.

Deer are social creatures. When hunters imitate some of the sounds they make, other deer may respond by approaching them. We may speculate about why they respond. It seems obvious why a buck would respond to a sound designed to imitate the bleats often made by does in heat. When the buck responds to our doe-in-heat calls by coming in and trying to mount the doe decoy in front of the stand, our theory about that would seem to be proven correct. When a buck approaches our stand in response to our buck grunts, and the buck walks in stiff-legged, ears back, in an apparently aggressive posture, we would be reasonable in supposing that the buck is responding to what he thinks is the challenge of another buck. In a similar vein, when we bawl like a fawn in

The sounds made by two bucks fighting, like these, attracts both bucks and does. Some may sneak in and others may come charging in! CREDIT TED ROSE.

distress, does tend to rush in on high alert, seemingly coming to the rescue of a fawn but very wary about the cause of the distress.

But why do does sometimes come in to the sound of bucks fighting? I have seen video footage of does, yearlings, and very small bucks rushing in from all points of the compass to watch two mature bucks fight. It reminds me of junior high school. Someone yells "Fight!" and instantly kids stop whatever they are doing and run over to see the action.

The fact is, deer are social creatures, and any deer may, depending on time of year and circumstances, come to investigate any sound that seems to emanate from another deer. Still, deer are more likely to respond to (and less likely to run from) the right call made at the right time. It's useful to have a basic understanding of the types of vocalizations deer make, and why they make them.

THE BASIC SOUNDS

I don't intend to go into great detail here attempting to represent, in print, what a specific deer vocalization sounds like, or to get into detailed instructions about how callers can best reproduce these sounds. Electronic media can do that far more effectively than can print media, and there is no shortage of television programs, hunting videos, and sound CDs available addressing the subject of calling deer. We can, however, distinguish what the basic deer vocalizations probably signify, and talk a little about the whys and whens of calling deer.

Among the more basic whitetail vocalizations is the doe blat or bleat. Not everyone agrees there is a difference, but many experienced hunters are convinced that the bleat is a higher pitched sound made by a fawn or a yearling, while the blat sounds much like the baa-aaa of a sheep or goat. Does seem to make this sound when they are separated from their fawns or from other deer that they have been traveling with, and are seeking to re-unite. A variation on this is the doe-in-heat blat, which is a longer, more drawn out, and more urgent blat.

Fawns will bleat for the same reasons does will blat–to reunite with their mother or their siblings when separated. When they are injured or threatened, they may bleat loudly and with great urgency, bawling in a high-pitched fashion. The sound can almost resemble an infant human crying. Anyone–even non-hunters–hearing this sound in the woods would instantly recognize it as some critter in distress, even if they didn't know what was making the sound.

Perhaps the call most familiar to deer hunters is the basic buck grunt, which is a sort of "beeerp" sound. From a distance, it can resemble the sound of a hog grunting. Bucks occasionally grunt, perhaps for some of the same reasons

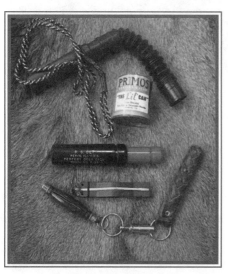

does blat. As the rut approaches and they begin cruising for does, they tend to grunt more often, and perhaps a little more urgently. These grunts may be warnings to other bucks in the areas. The buck that is closely following a doe that is in heat or about to come into heat often emits what is called a tending grunt–a series of grunts repeated one after another, often accompanied by a sort of ticking or clicking

There are many deer calls available to replicate the sounds deer make. Listen to some tapes or DVDs and practice your calls well in advance of the deer season so that you are comfortable when making a deer call. CREDIT FIDUCCIA ENTERPRISES.

sound. Sometimes, bucks close behind a doe will grunt with nearly every step. The buck making these sounds may be attempting to communicate to the doe, to cause her to stand for breeding, or again this may be a more urgent warning to other bucks nearby that this is his doe. A simple long, drawn-out grunt seems to be an aggressive sound directed at other bucks.

Snorts are a sound with which novice deer hunters quickly become familiar. The loud, often repetitive blowing sound is made by deer that have picked up the scent of a hunter. They run off snorting to warn any other deer of danger.

Tactics for "Talking" to Deer

How to effectively use grunt, blat, bleat, and snort calls

Includes
6
Action-Packed Hunts

Featuring Peter Fiduccia, the "Deer Doctor"

If you are new to using deer calls, it is a good idea to get a reliable video or DVD to listen to the various deer calls prior to heading afield and practicing with them on deer.
AVAILABLE AT WOODSNWATER.TV.

What many hunters don't realize is that this sound is not made exclusively by deer that have got a whiff of something they don't like. Sometimes a single snort seems to signify something more along the lines of "I'm over here, where are you?" Or perhaps it's "I'm over here, what are you?" In any case, an answering snort usually puts the deer at ease, and may even prompt it to move in the direction of the answering snort.

A sound that has gotten a lot of attention lately is the grunt-snort-wheeze, which seems to be an aggressive warning sound made by bucks, usually one buck warning another buck.

Sometimes some of these sounds are combined with other sounds. There are other variations on most of these sounds, probably with variations in meaning, too. Based on the behavior and body language of deer seen making these various sounds, it seems that generally speaking, the louder, more frequent, or more drawn out they are, the more emotion is conveyed, whether that emotion be fear, anger, or lust.

In addition to vocalizations of various kinds, deer communicate with non-vocal sounds. One of these is foot stomping. Deer sometimes do this as a warning to other deer. I've often observed deer doing this when they see something

Mitch Serlin, a seasoned whitetail hunter, puts one of his scents on to a ScentWrap on an overhanging branch. These self-wrapping wicks can also be placed at a specific distance from a stand and can stop a deer that comes in to check out the scent. CREDIT FIDUCCIA ENTERPRISES.

that disturbs them, or seems out of place, but they can't quite figure it out. It's sometimes done in conjunction with head bobbing. Decoys sometimes get this reaction, and one possible explanation for it is that deer are attempting to provoke whatever it is they are looking at into moving. If, in the course of this foot-stomping behavior, the object they're looking at moves, or (in the case of a hunter or other predator) if they catch its scent, they bolt instantly. As was noted in an earlier chapter, deer engaging in this behavior deposit scent from their interdigital glands, which may serve as a warning to other deer moving through the area.

We mentioned the sounds of bucks rubbing trees or thrashing around in saplings. Bucks engage in this sort of behavior with increasing frequency as the rut heats up, and may engage in it at any time. They are especially prone to do it, though, in the presence of other bucks, in an apparent attempt to intimidate them. In fact, bucks engage in all sorts of posturing, vocalizations, and other behaviors with the apparent attempt to intimidate other bucks. In the great majority of cases, this behavior does what it is intended to do–it establishes the dominance of one buck over another without the need for an all-out fight, which usually leads to the exhaustion of both bucks and often results in injuries, sometimes serious ones. Death resulting directly from a fight between two whitetail bucks is unusual. On the other hand, bucks lose much body weight and are in generally poorer shape after the rut is over. Winter mortality of bucks can be high, particularly in severe winters, and it is likely that fighting contributes indirectly to that mortality.

Far more frequent than all-out fights between bucks is sparring. Early in the season, these sparring matches seem almost playful or friendly, and perhaps they are. Later in the season they seem less friendly, but they still establish dominance without the need for a real fight. While it's unlikely the sounds of sparring or fighting are intended as communication, they have the effect of drawing deer (usually bucks), sometimes from long distances.

CHOOSING A CALL

There are calls on the market designed to imitate every one of the sounds we've discussed. Almost all of them will work, and various calls have their own advantages and disadvantages. For instance, some calls are highly adjustable, and can produce sounds ranging from the higher-pitched bleat of a yearling doe to the low-pitched grunt of a bruiser buck. The downside to these calls is more parts that can wear out or get lost over time. Simpler calls are less versatile, but often more durable.

Some calls require a little skill to operate, while others are virtually foolproof. The popular can-type calls are operated simply by turning them over, or pushing on the lid. Though not all hunters have a desire to use them, electronic calls of various sorts can be effective where legal. Some of these are operated by remote control, offering the advantage that the sound can emanate from the ground, as opposed to emanating from some unnatural place like twenty feet up a tree.

As a bowhunter, I like to keep movement to a minimum. At the same time, I worry about carrying a call around my neck, which might interfere with shooting. A number of calls are available that are very compact, and which can be held comfortably in the mouth, or which strap around the wrist of the shooting hand or clip to the collar. The idea with all these calls is that they can be used with minimal movement while the hunter is at full draw, and are unlikely to interfere with the shot.

Various devices are available for simulating the sound of rattling antlers. Some hunters insist on using nothing but real antlers, and are particular even down to the correct size of the antlers to be used. They pay a great deal of attention to the tone of the antlers, and try to preserve their antlers so that they don't dry out and change tone. Do deer really pay attention to the precise tonal quality of antlers clashing together?

Bucks have been known to rush in at people making sounds that only vaguely resemble rattling antlers. I have called in deer using real antlers, as well as a pair of "rattling sticks" made specifically to resemble antlers clashing, and have also used a couple of different rattling bags effectively. Rattling bags, if you haven't seen them, are small bags containing some loosely packed wooden sticks that, when shaken or rolled around, resemble the sounds of antlers clashing. None of these sounded exactly like the others.

Still, the human ear can detect the difference between, say, a pair of fresh antlers and a pair of antlers that have been lying around drying out for a few years. Presumably deer can hear the differences, too. Whether they respond better to one over the other I cannot say, but some of the best hunters I know are very particular about the sound they get from their antlers.

Assuming commercially made rattling devices such as rattling bags or

Big game hunter and CEO of Bookspan, Markus Wilhelm, always carries a grunt call with him on whitetail hunts. He is confident in being able to draw in bucks with a grunt on nearly every hunt. CREDIT FIDUCCIA ENTERPRISES.

rattling sticks work, their advantages are obvious. They do not normally dry out and change tone over time (though as I've indicated, whether or not this matters is debatable); and they are smaller and more compact, fitting easily into a day pack or fanny pack, and sometimes even a pocket. There is a safety factor, too. Some hunters are a little reluctant to be climbing around in trees with a pair of antlers around their neck or hanging off their backs. It's probably a good idea to hoist these up to the stand along with bows, guns, or daypacks. Every hunter using real antlers will sooner or later smack his fingers with the antlers, but that will probably only happen once.

The great thing about deer calls of any kind is that they are relatively simple devices, and almost all of them will work. Hunters should take into consideration their budgets, their specific needs, and their personal preferences, then purchase a call or two with confidence that, used correctly, it will work as intended.

USING CALLS

Some hunters are reluctant to use calls for fear that they will make a mistake and spook deer, instead of bringing them in. In my experience, deer often ignore calls, but they seldom are frightened by them. The only mistake most hunters calling deer need to concern themselves with, in my opinion, is calling deer that are too close. Two things are likely to happen. One is that the deer will pinpoint the source of the sound and see the caller. The other is that the deer will expect to see the deer that it thinks is making the sound and, when it doesn't, will get spooked and leave the area. The general rule of thumb is that when a hunter sees a deer responding to a call and heading his way, he stops calling. If the deer begins to move away, or its interest appears to flag, the hunter calls again. The idea is to call only as much as is necessary to bring the deer into range. The exception to that would be a call to stop a deer in a certain spot. Bowhunters in particular need a stationary or very slowly moving target. Many bowhunters always carry a grunt call for that purpose. Even on a day when they intend not to call, they will be prepared to grunt at a deer walking or running by in an attempt to make it stop momentarily in a shooting lane. It usually works.

Having said that, it is possible that does will shy away from buck grunts, or that a subordinate buck, or one that is exhausted from a recent fight, will be inclined to shy away from (or at least not respond to) the sound of another buck grunting, or the sounds of bucks sparring or fighting. It is impossible to say how often this happens. Only once have I ever had a deer turn and run at the sound of my call, and that was a doe that reacted that way when I belted out a fawn in distress bleat. I've used that same sound to call in quite a few does over the years, though.

Using calls that are appropriate for the kind of deer sought (buck or doe, trophy buck or any buck) only makes sense, but the fear of spooking deer by making an unrealistic sound, or by calling a little too often, is probably groundless. In fact, many experts are of the opinion that the biggest mistake inexperienced deer hunters make is not calling enough. Many very successful deer hunters recommend calling or (within two or three weeks of peak rut) doing rattling sequences every twenty or thirty minutes. Still others suggest calling as often as

Mitch Serlin, one of the principals of In-Scents, uses his grunt call every 20 to 30 minutes during the peak of the chase phase during the rut. CREDIT FIDUCCIA ENTERPRISES.

every five minutes, and rattling as often as every 15 minutes. The fact that they are all successful would suggest that the precise timing is not critical, and that calling frequently can be a successful tactic. The only caveat I would offer about frequent calling is this: every experienced deer hunter who does a lot of calling has been caught flat-footed at one time or another. The biggest buck I've ever seen in the woods was one that raced in seemingly out of nowhere to my rattling, and stopped only a few feet away from me, staring directly at me as I sat with my bow against a nearby tree and a pair of rattling antlers in my hands. Hunters who do any kind of calling must stay alert, and should alternate their calling sequences with periods of standing ready with bow or gun. Calling very frequently increases the likelihood that the hunter will be caught off guard, or that deer may spot the movements associated with calling.

One mistake novices sometimes make with regard to calling deer is not knowing when they have been successful. Although deer may charge in at full speed in response to a call, far more often than that they wander in taking their own sweet time. Because a deer moves by a stand 10 minutes after the last call was made does not mean that the deer is not responding to the call. Granted, the deer may have been coming that way call or no calls, and in a given instance we may never know for sure. I'm far from the only hunter, though, who has

Tag-teaming deer can be effective. One rattles or calls, the other shoots.

become convinced after years of experience that more deer "wander" by my stand when I've been calling then when I haven't.

Some hunters are concerned about rattling antlers up in a tree, since this is not a location from which deer would normally be sparring or fighting. There are ways to get around that problem. Some hunters tie antlers to a rope and lower them to the ground. By pulling on the rope, they can rattle the answers on the ground.

Another option, of course, is to hunt with a buddy, and take turns rattling. This approach makes a lot of sense, because bucks responding to rattling are often nervous. They tend to be on high alert, and sometimes rush in, stop for a moment, and then rush out. The bowhunter who is holding a rattling device instead of his bow is going to miss some hard-won opportunities.

Finally, though we have discussed calling, use of scents, and decoying in separate chapters, that is not meant to suggest that they must be entirely separate things. Most hunters combine calling with scent use, or decoys, or both, and it only stands to reason that the methods can complement one another.

Mike Gallop, one of the principals of In-Scents, believes in the combination of scents and rattling to bring deer in close. CREDIT FIDUCCIA ENTERPRISES.

Connecticut bowhunter Mike Gallop, who manufactures In-Scents hunting products that include cover and attractant scents, often calls deer in conjunction with the use of his scents. He prefers to use drag rags to bring deer in from distances, and positions scent wicks to maneuver deer into open shooting lanes. Mike also calls and rattles deer, and on a recent hunt Mike put out a scent wick, then began rattling. It wasn't long before he rattled in a nice Connecticut five-point buck.

"I missed it," Mike concedes. "I just plain . . . missed it. It ran off, probably wondering what had happened. It was getting close to the peak of the rut, though, and he was interested in that doe in heat scent. In fact, he turned around, came back, and gave me a second shot."

Mike made good on his second opportunity and tagged the buck. It's not often that hunters get a second chance at a good whitetail, but appealing to more than one sense at a time, as Mike did with scent and rattling, certainly improves the chances.

The bottom line on calling deer is that hunters should not be afraid to use their calls. Often, deer will ignore them. They have their own agendas, their own schedules, and their own travel routes, and they will not always alter these because they hear what they think is another deer making sounds elsewhere in the woods.

Some deer may on occasion shy away from certain calls, or even run from them. In my experience, that doesn't happen often. And calls do work. Sometimes they work dramatically. Like decoys, food plots, or scent products, they don't work every time. If they did, they would have to be outlawed. They are a useful and sometimes exciting addition to the deer hunter's bag of tricks. ■

Mike Gallop uses a mix of buck urine and tarsal gland scent on a drag rag on his way to his whitetail stand. CREDIT FIDUCCIA ENTERPRISES.

CREATING MOCK SCRAPES AND RUBS

I f hunters are to have any hope of effectively creating mock scrapes and rubs, they must have a thorough understanding of what scrapes and rubs are, and how deer use them. The fact is, there is still a great deal we don't know about the subject. Biologists are gathering information continually, though, and in recent years some good, scientific studies have been undertaken that have enriched our knowledge and resulted in some surprising insights. Like all good scientific studies, they have also raised new questions.

We've looked at scrapes previously, but this might be a good place to review a more or less conventional way of looking at scrapes. In the weeks leading up to the peak of the rut, bucks, especially mature bucks, paw away leaves, sticks, and any debris on the ground to expose fresh earth. They then stand over the exposed area and rub-urinate, a behavior that entails rubbing together the tarsal glands on the hind legs and urinating over them into the scrape. This deposits urine, along with any tarsal gland secretions, into the scrape. Does will visit the scrapes, and bucks will return at intervals to freshen the scrapes and check to see if does have visited. When they detect the scent of a doe that is in or approaching estrous, they will then take up the trail.

"Serious" scrapes–that is, scrapes that are likely to be visited regular-ly–always have a licking branch overhead at a height that is easy for the buck to reach. (Licking "twig" might be a more descriptive term, since they are usual-ly the very ends of small branches.) Bucks will rub their forehead and

Finding a scrape like this one always gets the blood pumping in anticipation of finding out what buck made it! CREDIT FIDUCCIA ENTERPRISES.

pre-orbital glands against these licking branches, presumably depositing glandular scent on them, and will also lick and chew on them, depositing saliva.

Scrapes at particularly desirable locations may become "signpost" scrapes. These scrapes will be used by more than one buck, and will become enlarged, sometimes to the size of garbage can lids or bigger.

A few decades ago, when hunters first began to understand the nature of scrapes and what they signified, they understandably became excited. The thinking was something like this: Here is fresh sign, created by a mature buck, and he visits this spot regularly looking for does. All I've got to do now is put my stand up downwind from this scrape and wait for Mr. Big to come along.

If the scrape was a very large, signpost scrape, that was even more exciting. Not one buck, but a number of bucks were using the scrape.

Among the first observations hunters made after a few years of scrape hunting was that bucks didn't always go directly to scrapes, but often seemed to scent check them from some distance downwind. That required the relatively simple adjustment of moving the stands farther downwind from the scrape.

Perhaps an even earlier, more frequently made observation, was that bucks weren't visiting the scrapes at all during the many hours hunters spent watching them from nearby tree stands. Scrape hunting, it turned out, was not a route to guaranteed success. But how could this be? The scrapes were fresh, and in some cases showed regular activity. Clearly, the scrapes were being visited at night.

WHAT SCIENCE SAYS

As biologists began studying the phenomenon of scrapes and scraping activity, they began putting together more pieces of the puzzle. Some of the early studies, instructive as they were, later proved flawed with regard to certain behaviors, for a very simple reason: they were based on observations of captive deer, in many cases only during daylight hours. Captive deer, as it turned out, did not always exhibit the same behaviors as free-ranging deer, nor did deer behave the same during the day as during the night.

Two more recent studies have greatly added to the store of knowledge about scrapes. The first was a two-year study completed in the fall of 1999, and was reported by wildlife biologist Karen Alexy of the Quality Deer Management Association in Watkinsville, Georgia. Alexy's team installed motion-activated video cameras to observe the behavior of a population of free-ranging deer at a 3,460-acre location in northeast Georgia.

The team located six active scrapes sites, four along field edges and two in forests, and placed the video cameras near the scrapes. Flood lights with red lenses were programmed to turn on at night. The results of this study confirmed some of what was already believed true, but also offered some surprises.

One unsurprising result confirmed what hunters were already beginning to suspect: 85 percent of all scraping activity occurred at night. (Actually, some hunters might have guessed the number would be higher.)

More surprisingly, while previous research on captive deer suggested that only dominant bucks perform all the behaviors associated with scraping activity, the Georgia study indicated that many bucks worked the same scrapes, including yearling bucks, and that they engaged in all the scraping activities that the mature bucks engaged in.

Does were often seen visiting scrapes, sometimes using licking branches, but since the researchers were unable to distinguish one doe from another, it was impossible to tell how often a given doe visited a scrape, or whether a given scrape was visited repeatedly by the same doe or by a number of different does.

It was no surprise that most of the scraping activity occurred in the two-to-three-week period leading up to the rut, and that scraping activity dropped off sharply after the peak of the rut.

While some scrapes were visited by as many as 13 bucks, others were visited by only a few. An even bigger surprise was that two of the scrapes that were less than 300 yards apart were visited by entirely different groups of bucks, with only one buck visiting both groups of scrapes. One conclusion the researchers reached was that the notion of a single buck creating a scrape line seemed unlikely.

The area under study was hunted, which led to an interesting side note: hardly any of the mature bucks of 3 1/2 years or older that were taken by

Every real scrape includes a licking branch. Here, hunter adds a forehead gland scent to a licking branch before climbing into his stand.

hunters during the two-year period were ever seen on video, though several of them were taken within a few hundred yards of scrapes being monitored. The researchers speculated these bucks may have been monitoring the scrapes from downwind.

A less exciting, but possibly very useful bit of information is that bucks visited scrapes far more often than they marked them with rub-urinating or use of licking branches. The researchers suspect this indicates that the scents left at the scrapes endure for fairly long periods of time, so it is not necessary for bucks to mark them frequently.

During roughly the same time period that this study was being undertaken, the Institute for White-tailed Deer Management and Research studied deer reactions to mock scrapes. Research Associate Ben Koerth set up the mock scrapes on an 8,000-acre hunting club in East Texas during the pre-rut period of late October, using a variety of approaches. These included 1) no scent, 2) mock scrapes with rutting buck scent, 3) mock scrapes with doe-in-heat scent, 4) mock scrapes with a combination of rutting buck and doe-in-heat scent, 5) rutting buck scent on the ground with no mock scrape, and 6) doe-in-heat scent on the ground with no mock scrape. These various scent stations were monitored by infrared-triggered cameras. A total of 25 stations were monitored, five for each type of scent.

The results were interesting, beginning with the observation that the various scent stations did in fact attract deer. Does and fawns were attracted to the scrapes, but the majority of visits were from bucks.

Before you get too excited, though, consider the other observations. First, deer showed almost no inclination to revisit a scrape after they discovered it. Only one buck was observed to revisit the same mock scrape, and he did it one time, five days after his first visit. Further, only one buck visited more than one of the 25 mocks scrapes in the area.

Koerth's study revealed several other interesting bits of information. For one thing, he put his his scrapes in areas of high traffic, that he thought were sure to yield quick results. When several of the scrapes got no visitors, he found that by moving them only a few feet, he soon began to get photographs of deer visiting those locations.

Another useful observation: deer visiting the scrapes did not spend a great deal of time at them. They stopped briefly and moved on.

With regard to which types of scents received the most visitations, the main distinction appeared to be between the mock scrapes made in conjunction with scents, and the scents applied alone, without the scrapes. While deer visited all the stations Koerth created, they were more inclined to visit those using a combination of the scrape and the scent. This strongly suggests that scrapes are visual, as well as olfactory cues.

Also of interest, in a follow-up study Koerth used human urine, buck urine, and doe-in-heat urine in mock scrapes, and discovered that deer came to the human urine as readily as to either of the other scents.

Koerth's conclusions with regard to the use of scents and mock scrapes, were as follows: Scrapes and scents can be useful to hunters. Deer probably react to them mostly from curiosity. They will move a short distance to investigate them when they encounter them, but are unlikely to respond to them from long distances, and are unlikely to change their normal travel patterns to approach them. Their best use is probably to bring deer that pass near them into a shooting position, and stop them there just long enough to enable an alert hunter to get off a shot.

Like all good studies, Koerth's raises almost as many questions as it answers. The study was not intended, as Koerth concedes in his report, to compare one commercially produced scent product to another. Instead, he simply went out and purchased the first scents he encountered, assuming he could buy it in sufficient quantities to use the same scent for all his scent stations. This raises one very important if obvious question: could other scents, perhaps because of better initial quality, better quality control, or greater freshness, have produced better results?

Another issue: Koerth observed, as have some other researchers, that moving the stations for distances as little as a few feet made an immediate and dramatic difference in the numbers of deer visiting that station. What is not clear is why changing the location by such a small amount made such a difference. The assumption is that deer were not willing to change their travel patterns by even a short distance, but perhaps there were other reasons. We don't know if, for instance, the original mock scrapes lacked a licking branch overhead. If so, simply moving the scrape a short distance to a location with a licking branch

Hunter adds scent to a mock scrape he has made in a logging road.

overhead might be the reason for the increased visitation, as opposed to the new scrape being closer to a habitual path of travel. Licking branches aside, there might be other factors we are not aware of that cause deer to prefer one location to another for scrapes.

Another question is raised by the limitation of the cameras being used. If it's true that bucks often travel downwind of scrapes, scent checking them from a distance, is it not possible–perhaps even likely–that bucks that visited a scrape one time were not photographed repeatedly because they tended to scent check it from downwind after the initial visit?

All these questions and more might be answered by future studies, but in the meantime, we can theorize that the use of mock scrapes and scents might be analogous to the situation of bringing an animal to a call. Experienced turkey hunters, for instance, are well aware that it is much easier to call a turkey to a place the bird wants to go to. That does not mean calling isn't effective, it simply means that the location from which the call is made is an important factor in the likelihood of successfully calling in a turkey.

HOW IT'S DONE

Certainly many hunters use them, and some excellent hunters swear by them. Creating the mock scrape itself is as simple as scraping up debris to expose bare earth, then applying any of several types of deer urine or, as increasing numbers of hunters are doing, urinating in the scrape themselves. Naturally hunters will want to take extra care to avoid contaminating the spot with their own scent, including wearing rubber gloves.

The more complex aspect of creating an effective mock scrape is choosing a suitable location. Hunters like Ben Koerth have observed that moving a mock scrape even a short distance can make the difference between deer using the scrape or not using it. Beyond positioning the mock scrape along a route that deer want to use anyway, another key factor is the licking branch. It's usually a waste of time to establish a mock scrape in a spot lacking a licking branch overhead.

That doesn't necessarily mean that hunters must look around for a licking branch before thinking about making a scrape. In fact, one of the more effective techniques hunters have hit upon in developing mock scrapes is to cut off the licking branch over a real scrape, and position it over a spot where a mock scrape is to be made. Not only is the lack of a licking branch resolved, but the licking branch put in place is one containing the natural scent deposited by bucks.

Why not simply hunt over the real scrape? It might be in a spot lacking suitable trees for a stand, for one thing. Or the trees that would otherwise be suitable might be upwind of the prevailing breeze. Or the location might be difficult to access, or in a valley with swirling breezes, or too close to a bedding area, or less than ideal for any number of reasons. By creating a mock scrape, the hunter is attempting to influence a buck to come to a particular spot that the hunter finds advantageous, as opposed to hunting a spot that might leave the buck with all the advantages.

Many hunters believe it's important to keep a scrape fresh, which means freshening it regularly, at least every few days. There's an easier way, though and it might solve several problems at once. By using a scrape dripper, most of which release scent as the temperature rises, hunters can avoid the necessity of repeatedly visiting a scrape to freshen it. Scrape drippers are widely available at sporting goods stores as well as in hunting supply catalogs, and there are two additional advantages to using drippers. First, since hunters needn't repeatedly approach the scrape to freshen it, they avoid the possibility of contaminating it with foreign odors. Finally, as we've observed most scrape activity, including simply scent-checking scrapes, occurs at night. There is little doubt that deer can determine how much time has elapsed since scent was deposited in a scrape. It is possible that by releasing scent into the scrape only during daylight hours, a buck can be influenced over time to check the mock scrape during the day.

Wicks can be hung from limbs or licking branches to disperse scent. They rarely draw deer from great distances, but they can distract deer and help move them into perfect shooting position.

RUBS

Perhaps even more exciting to deer hunters than a fresh scrape is a fresh rub, especially if the rub is on a large tree. More so than large tracks or even scrapes, rubs are clearly the work of bucks. And while large bucks will often rub saplings or small trees, it is unusual for a small buck to rub a tree with the girth of, say, a telephone pole. A rub on any tree with a diameter of 8 inches or more was almost surely made by a big buck, particularly if the tree is deeply scored.

As with scrapes, rubs are both a visual and an olfactory cue for deer. Bucks deposit the scent from their forehead and pre-orbital glands in rubs, but rubs are even more visible than are scrapes. In areas where vegetation is not overly thick, a rub can be seen for long distances through the woods. In heavily traveled areas including funnels, staging areas near food sources, or bedding areas, hunters can sometimes stand in one spot and see numerous rubs, or a line of rubs trailing off into the forest.

While I've yet to come across a scientific study of rubs or mock rubs, anecdotal evidence suggests that mock rubs can work. As is the case with scrapes, location is critical. Bucks simply are not going to take a route they are not naturally inclined to take just to investigate a new rub, though they will certainly travel a short distance to check it out, and may provide an excellent shot opportunity as they pause to investigate it.

Most hunters who create mock rubs use a simple file to rub off the bark. (Keep in mind that this practice will likely be illegal in public hunting areas, and should be done only with the permission of landowners.) Several companies offer forehead gland scent compounds of one sort or another to use on mock rubs as well as licking branches over scrapes. Naturally, hunters want to wear rubber gloves and take the usual precautions to avoid contaminating a mock rub area with their own scent.

HOW TWO SUCCESSFUL HUNTERS USE MOCK SCRAPES

Some hunters are so sold on the use of mock scrapes that they begin using them months prior to the rut. I know of at least one case of a hunter who uses them year-round. The effectiveness of what they are doing might be controversial, but these hunters are not off the wall, and can present perfectly defendable reasoning for what they do. While biologists point out that scraping activity generally begins in earnest a few weeks prior to the rut, and tapers off rapidly after the peak of the rut, they are talking about the entire package of scraping behavior. Scraping is essentially a marking behavior, and the fact is that deer–bucks and does–engage in some marking behaviors year round. They make occasional scrapes, if they're not as obvious as scrapes made during the rut, and they frequently tend to nuzzle and lick branches. And, of course, they urinate. These behaviors allow deer to keep tabs on other deer in the area, probably telling them something about the health and social status of these deer.

Once you find a natural rub in a given area, make your own mock rub on a similarly sized tree not too far away. CREDIT FIDUCCIA ENTERPRISES.

When making a mock scrape, it is important to keep your human scent to a minimum. Use a stick to clear the area of leaves, grass or other woodland debris.
CREDIT FIDUCCIA ENTERPRISES.

Be sure to add some buck urine to a mock scrape. When a buck comes into the area to wind check his own scrape, he will smell the odor of the "competing buck," which will agitate him to check it out. CREDIT FIDUCCIA ENTERPRISES.

Dan Parrot is a bottler/distributor of deer scents, not to mention a long-time deer hunter. Dan lives in central Ohio, not far from where the world-record Beatty Buck was taken. For years, Dan has begun creating mock scrapes in mid-to-late summer, and he is convinced that he sees more trophy bucks on his hunting property as a result.

Dan's theory–and there is scientific evidence supporting it–is that does can distinguish mature, healthy, dominant bucks from lesser bucks, that does seek out dominant bucks, and will gravitate to areas where dominant bucks live, at least in areas where the herd is healthy and relatively well-balanced. As the rut approaches, bucks seek out does. Dan believes that his early mock scrapes with dominant buck urine attract and hold does, which in turn attract and hold dominant bucks as the rut approaches. Developing hard, scientific evidence to prove Dan's theory would be difficult, but it's hard to argue with success, and Dan has certainly taken his share of big bucks over the years.

The relative effectiveness of mock scrapes and rubs continues to be a controversial subject. The limited amount of truly scientific studies examining scrapes and mock scrapes reveals some interesting information, but one or two studies can never be conclusive, and they leave many questions unanswered. At the very least, it seems clear that deer, including mature bucks, will often stop to investigate a mock scrape they encounter. Since mock scrapes can be strategically placed, this could provide a hunter with a shot opportunity he might not otherwise have. How many hunters would be willing to create a mock scrape just to increase the odds of a close, broadside shot at a buck moving by his stand? My guess is that any hunter who has ever had a really good buck move past his stand within range but without offering a good shot opportunity would be inclined to give it serious consideration. And if hunters like Dan Parrot are right, mock scrapes can do more than simply cause a buck to stop in a shooting lane. ■

Waterholes, whether natural or man-made (like this one at Bluff Country Outfitters in Wisconsin), are good areas to create mock rubs or scrapes. CREDIT FIDUCCIA ENTERPRISES.

MANIPULATING HABITAT

omewhere in our dim and ancient past, a hunter hiding patiently in a deadfall broke off a few limbs to create an opening through which he could better see approaching game. Eventually, some descendent of that same hunter dragged a deadfall to a waterhole or game trail to serve as a blind. When modern hunters hang stands in trees, or put up ground blinds to fool the eyes, ears, or nose of game, they are manipulating habitat. The senderos of the Southwest attract game and provide shooting lanes, and more than a few Midwestern hunters maintain logging roads for no other purpose than to create travel lanes for wildlife, as well as easy, quiet access for hunters. With the right tools and a little time, it's not that difficult for hunters to create travel lanes that deer will use regularly. Deer, like most animals (not to mention humans) tend instinctively to follow the path of least resistance. By clearing some timber in thick, second-growth areas, and arranging the cut timber to further funnel deer movement patterns, hunters can take advantage of wind direction, thermals, or trees that lend themselves well to permanent or portable stands to provide more and better shot opportunities.

On my Ohio hunting lease, I've placed flat rocks across a stream at two different crossing spots. No, the deer don't use them–I do. The creek bisects the property, and after a couple of seasons of splashing across in the dark when the stream was high, or clattering across on loose rocks when the creek was low, it occurred to me to place the flat stones strategically to solve the problem. Now I can cross the stream without making a sound, even in the predawn darkness.

More often associated with food plots or mock scrapes, rakes can be very

Food plots can be planted by hand, by ATV, and by tractor. This field will be planted in no time at all with the tractor and LandPride seeder and compactor attachment. CREDIT FIDUCCIA ENTERPRISES.

useful for manipulating habitat in another way, too. Walking in dry leaves creates a racket that can be heard over long distances on a still day. Savvy hunters can use rakes to get leaves off the trail leading to their stands, as well as raking them away from the area immediately under their stand, so they can approach it in dry weather without alerting deer. Whitetail authority Peter Fiduccia introduced this tactic in 1983. At the time, some found the tactic a lot of work. That is until they realized how effective it really was in getting to deer stands quietly and undiscovered by deer. In some instances, it enables hunters to actually walk up on deer that otherwise would have heard their approach and have disappeared into cover long before the hunter arrived. With the development of leaf blowers, clearing trails has become even less of a job than it was years ago.

Among the more common ways that modern hunters manipulate deer habitat is putting in food plots. The primary purposes of food plots include attracting and holding game, and improving the quality of the game, but the hunter who establishes food plots without giving careful thought to how he can design, locate, and modify food plots in a way that will prevent game from catching his scent, seeing him, or hearing him approach, is not getting the full benefits of his hard work.

A tremendous amount of research and experimentation has gone into developing effective food plots, and there is a growing army of entrepreneurs, wildlife biologists, hunting lodge managers, outfitters, and just plain hunters with expertise in the area. While the specifics of how to put in food plots and what kind of foods to plant are beyond the scope of this book, the best planning in the world will be time wasted if the food plot fails to attract deer. Not all foods are equally attractive to deer at a given time, and hunters need to give some consideration to planting the foods that do well in their area, as well as a mix of foods that will be attractive to deer at various times throughout the hunting season. Some plants–chufa is one–are very attractive to deer, but tend to do best in the deep South. Steve Gruber of Frigid Forage, on the other hand, specializes in producing food plot products that are geared toward hunters in temperate and northern areas such as the Midwest and the Northeast. Gruber has also created mixes designed specifically to insure that deer are attracted to food plots year-round, and particularly through the hunting season. Some of Gruber's mixes include some plants more often associated with gardens than with food plots.

"There's a reason it's so hard to keep deer out of backyard vegetable gardens," Steve explains. "The reason is, deer love vegetables. So we give them vegetables. Some of our mixes include not only the more traditional clovers, chicories, or rapes, but carrots, turnips, peas, and beets. Deer love that stuff."

The father-son team of Craig and Neil Dougherty are among those who have learned not only to develop excellent food plots, but to design them in such a way as to influence deer travel patterns while allowing hunters to approach and hunt from them undetected. The Doughertys' Habitat and Hunting Development Demo Center in upstate New York is a 500-acre plot of ground that has produced some book bucks in an area once almost totally devoid of them.

While there are a number of good reasons for hunters to establish food plots, certainly one of the main goals is to provide hunters with shot opportunities at more or bigger deer. Deer are happy enough to take advantage of food plots, but they prefer to avoid offering shot opportunities, and their most important defense mechanism, as we've seen, is their nose. Deer that detect the presence of a hunter near or over a food plot not only avoid that area at that time, but they learn quickly to associate danger with that food plot, or at least the area near the stand. Deer visit the plot less frequently, and when they do they are very wary. If they detect the scent of the hunter more than a couple of times, they'll continue to use the food plot–but only at night.

The first and most obvious way to address the problem is to put stands on the downwind side of food plots. (Or better still, put stands on either side of a plot to make the spot huntable regardless of wind direction.) That leaves several problems, though, including the possibility that deer will approach the plot from a downwind direction. Strategically locating food plots downwind from likely bedding areas can help, though in some circumstances deer may shift bedding areas to be downwind of the food plot.

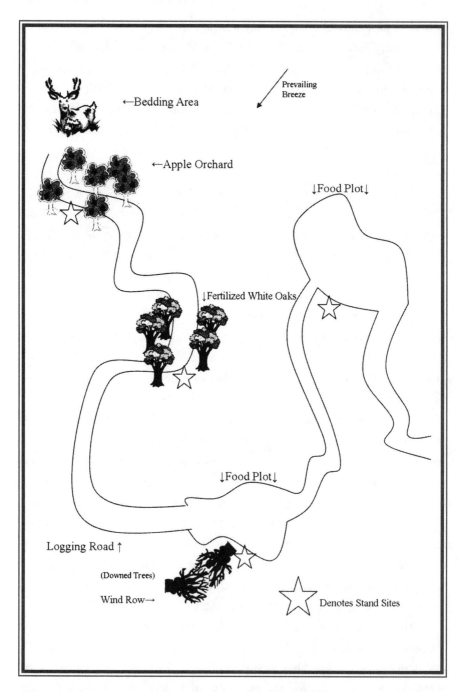

Prevailing
Breeze

←Bedding Area

←Apple Orchard

↓Food Plot↓

↓Fertilized White Oaks↓

↓Food Plot↓

Logging Road ↑

(Downed Trees)

Wind Row→

Denotes Stand Sites

By supplementing existing food sources, fertilizing native plants, creating a trail or path, and planting several small food plots, all with wind direction in mind, hunters can not only improve the quality of their deer herd, but also greatly increase their chances of good shooting opportunities. CREDIT PC FIDUCCIA.

Brassicas are a hardy crop to plant that provide forage for deer into the cold winter months. This particular blend contains plants that deer love: Sugar Beets, Purple Top Forage Turnip, Carrots, Winfred Forage Rape, Dwarf Essex Rape, and Hunter Forage Rape/Turnip Hybrid. CREDIT FRIGID FORAGE/SUN RICH FARMS.

Neil Dougherty scouted his New York property extensively enough to learn where the deer bedded, and the travel routes they generally followed, and laid out a series of food plots consisting of large and small plots. The larger plots he considered nutrition plots, though these could be hunted effectively in firearms seasons. A portion of the property was designated as a sanctuary–an area including ideal bedding habitat, as well as a larger food plot or two. The idea was to provide the deer with an area on the property where they felt safe, to keep them on the property. Larger plots were developed elsewhere, too. These plots drew large numbers of deer, and some could be hunted effectively, at least during firearms season. Neil learned that deer tend to be warier about entering larger plots, preferring in some cases to enter them in low light conditions, or after dark. Deer are less wary about smaller plots of an acre or less, located close to bedding areas and in areas surrounded by protective cover. These smaller plots are also much better for bowhunters, since deer using them are much more likely to come into bow range.

In the case of both larger and smaller plots, Neil found he could influence the travel patterns of deer using the plots by laying out the plots in an irregular shape, usually with a choke point near the middle of the plot. A simple hour glass shape served that function. He also learned that a turn in the plot would often bring deer to a predictable location in the plot, since the deer preferred to move to an area from which they could see around the turn, to spot other deer or potential danger.

Going a step beyond this, he observed natural trails and choke points, and even created some of his own, by clearing logging roads through thickets or past attractive oak trees, apple trees, or other food sources that attracted deer. By developing food plots with all this in mind, he eventually created a situation in which deer would move along a relatively predictable route that would take them along known trails and through a series of small food plots along the way.

He wasn't done yet, though. He soon discovered that no matter how carefully he laid out the food plots, mature deer tended to circle to the downwind side of the plots before entering them. Since Neil used tractors or bulldozers to create many of the food plots, he hit on the idea of creating windrows. By simply pushing downed trees into an elongated pile on the downwind side of his stand, he could make it inconvenient, if not impossible, for deer to circle directly downwind of his stand.

Not everyone has the equipment needed to create huge, elongated, and carefully placed trees and brush to an extent that will prevent deer from moving through an area. Putting up fences can work on a temporary basis. In most cases at least two strands of fence are needed to discourage deer from easily going over or under these constructions.

Neil's final touch was to place licking branches or mock scrapes along the plot edge at the choke point of his hour glass, in front of the stand. He now had a spot that gave deer, including mature bucks, numerous reasons to be within bow range of his stand, upwind, during daylight hours.

Lest you fear that Neil created a "controlled" deer herd that guaranteed his success, keep in mind that deer outside a fence are never going to follow the same route on a daily basis, and the situation is never static–deer behavior will always be influenced by changing cover from year to year and even within a season, by when acorns, apples, or other food sources are ripe, when nearby crops are harvested, and even from one day to the next by weather. Neil was not seeking to control deer activity, but he was able to become one of the many influences of their behavior to an extent that increased his hunting success.

Hunters who think they can't attract deer or improve the quality of the local deer unless they can create food plots are making a mistake. One of my hunting buddies prefers to pay farmers to leave patches of corn, soybeans, alfalfa, etc. standing in strategic areas. The farmer is happy, my friend is happy, and he saves time and money. While this approach lacks some of the year-round benefits of dedicated food plots, my friend lives in an area that produces huge bucks anyway. The crops left in place are deer magnets during portions of the hunting season, especially since they are the only remaining crops after surrounding crops are harvested.

Deer, turkey, and other wild animals benefit from sunflowers. The seeds are nutritious and the tall plants also provide great cover. CREDIT FIDUCCIA ENTERPRISES.

If there are old pear trees on the property you hunt, fertilize them in the early spring and again in the fall to help produce better fruit. CREDIT FIDUCCIA ENTERPRISES.

Woods N' Water television host, Peter Fiduccia, has been manipulating habitat since at least as early as the mid 1980s. Among Peter's earlier projects on his hunting property was planting pine trees. Pine trees are far from a preferred food for whitetails, but Peter wasn't planting them as a food source. He was planting them primarily because they provide cover. Providing extra cover encourages deer to spend more time on the property–in some cases, providing extra cover for security and bedding areas is a more effective way to hold deer in an area than is planting food for them.

Peter addressed the issue of food, too, but not only in the form of food plots. All the oaks on his property were red oaks, for instance, and Peter knew that, given the choice, deer generally prefer the acorns of white oaks. He bought some white oak trees that were about 15 feet tall and planted them in strategic locations. He also bought fruit trees, again in the 10 to 15 foot height range, along with chestnuts, dogwoods, and other food sources that deer prize whenever the fruit is ripe.

Peter was also among the first deer hunters to recognize the advantages of fertilizing non-crop foods. "A lot of people see wild grape vines in the woods and think it's poison ivy or some other type of vine. Because the grapes are usually growing high up on the vine, to get as much sun light as possible, they wind up high in the trees where most hunters don't realize their presence. The grapes are rarely noticed on the ground because a majority of the time they are eaten by birds, squirrels, and other critters long before they even fall off the vine. Once they hit the ground, they are almost instantly consumed by deer, bear, turkey, or other wildlife. If you locate a wild grapevine and fertilize it, trim away some of the surrounding undergrowth, and even some branches on the tree. You will provide the vine more light, which in turn will produce larger, sweeter and more abundant grapes. Interestingly, the more you fertilize the plant and provide more sunlight, the quicker the vine begins to produce grape clusters lower on the vine, where deer can reach them. Everything likes wild grapes–deer, bear turkeys, grouse, they'll all eat them without hesitation."

Existing trees can be fertilized to good advantage, and with faster results than planting new trees. Tree fertilizer spikes–widely available at garden or home improvement centers–are relatively inexpensive and easy to use. A fertilized oak, for instance, will provide more mast, and mast that will be higher in protein than nearby unfertilized oaks. This is a great way to get more nutrition to deer, but it also attracts deer to the spot, since they can taste the difference and will prefer the acorns that are higher in protein. Peter also noticed that fertilizing oaks not only produces bigger, sweeter and more abundant acorns–but the healthier mast tends to fall much later than non-fertilized trees, providing a longer lasting mast crop for your deer. Peter suggests fertilizing oaks and other vegetation in the spring and again in the autumn for best results.

One of the quickest and most effective ways to improve deer habitat is as simple as clearing trees with a chainsaw. Most of us have an instinctive reluctance to crank up a chain saw and begin lopping off trees, but used judiciously they can create openings that 1) create food, since new growth is nutritious and easily within the reach of deer, and 2) create cover and bedding areas, first in the form of deadfalls and later as new growth becomes thick, second growth.

We mentioned the use of fence lines to prevent deer from circling downwind of food plots, but where fences already exist (and where allowed) hunters can create openings in fences to influence travel routes.

Controlled burns are yet another way to create openings and new growth that will attract deer and other species of wildlife. Many county agricultural agencies, and some divisions of wildlife, have experts on hand who can advise, or in some cases even help with, controlled burns to improve wildlife habitat.

Ponds attract wildlife of all kinds, including deer. In more arid regions, any waterhole can be an instant hotspot, but even in less arid regions, ponds create habitat that attracts deer. In particularly dry or cold weather, deer need water more often, and will visit ponds to get water. They also like the cover and the vegetation that grows around ponds. Then too, ponds in an area that otherwise attracts deer, or on a travel route that deer routinely use can, like other structures, tend to funnel them along certain more predictable routes. I'm thinking of a ladder stand against an old oak beside a pond on the Kentucky hunting lease of a good friend of mine. A finger of trees extends from a wooded hillside up to the pond, beside which runs a logging road. On the other side of the pond a similar finger of trees extends up from the opposite slope, stopping at the logging road. It's a natural crossing point, and deer must skirt the pond to cross there. I was fortunate enough to take a very respectable eight-pointer from that stand a few years ago, and over the years it has been a consistent producer of good bucks. Being forced to skirt the pond is what puts the deer in bow range.

No doubt there are other ways hunters can alter habitat to their advantage. The only way to be sure, though, that the alterations are truly to the advantage of the hunter, and not the deer, is to plan habitat modifications with wind direction, scent control, and easy, quiet access in mind. ■

ZEN DEER HUNTING

It's not very original of me, I suppose, to include this chapter in my book on deer hunting. In my book *Advanced Turkey Hunting,* I included a chapter entitled "Zen Turkey Hunting". The thing is, I believe in it. I am not a mystically inclined person. My friends will tell you that I tend toward skepticism, and I suspect folks who know me but harbor less friendly feelings toward me would say I am cynical. I do believe, though, that the very best hunters are people who become so totally immersed in their surroundings, and so totally engaged in the hunt, that they reach a stage of hyper alertness, in which they see and hear in a way that other people who are not at that level of alertness cannot see or hear. In fact, all their senses are heightened. I don't believe in any sort of "sixth sense," but hunters operating at this level almost seem to possess it.

Part of it has to do with forgetting the clock. For animals, I suspect, life is pretty much right now. They have memories, and they are capable of learning. Certainly they may be affected by their past. But they experience life in the here and now, neither agonizing over past behaviors nor worrying about the future. There is no place they have to be. There is nothing they "should" be doing.

We humans–Americans in particular–have elevated the desire for productivity to the level of a moral value. We feel guilty if we're not using every moment productively, and even if we are, we worry that there is something else we could be doing that might be an even more productive use of our time. We have cell phones, pagers, fax machines, and computers, "time saving" devices that not only enable us to work anywhere, any time, but create the expectation that we will. Then we worry–all too often with justification–that we aren't spending enough time with our families. We work more and more and worry more and more and suffer the consequences more and more. Obesity, diabetes, high blood pressure, heart disease, depression, and other stress-related illnesses reach higher and higher numbers each year.

On top of all that, most of us spend the greater part of our lives in boxes. Our houses are boxes, our vehicles are boxes, our workplaces are boxes. We view the world through glass from what amounts to an artificial womb. For millions of us, caring for our lawns and playing an occasional round of golf is as close as we get to experiencing the outdoors. About eight miles from my suburban home is a 100-acre fenced-in area called the Nature Center. I've been a member on and off for years. It's a great thing. Busloads of kids come out from the inner city, not to mention the nearby suburbs, to walk around looking at "nature." Signs warn them not to stray from the carefully manicured trail. They wander about like astronauts on the moon, staring at trees and meadows, looking for "wildlife." In the unlikely event they should see a deer, they are equally divided between two reactions: those who fear it will attack them, and those who want to go pet it.

Not all of us are quite that removed from nature, but few of us are unaffected by the reality just described. Most of us enter the woods handicapped by a heavy burden, and I'm not talking about our climbing stand, our daypack, our blind, or any of the other paraphernalia we hunt with. I'm talking about our workaday stress, about the conflict we're having with a boss or co-worker, about deadlines, about bills, about the room we could be painting, the plumbing we could be fixing, or the car we could be repairing. If we are to hunt effectively, enjoy our time afield (and, by the way, fully achieve the health benefits of getting outdoors, getting a little exercise, and getting our minds off our problems), we must shuck all that stuff and leave the modern world behind.

Years ago, on an opening day bowhunt out of a lodge in Mississippi, an elderly guide sat behind the wheel of a pick-up truck driving me down a logging road to my stand. He was a quiet old guy, who rarely put more than two or three words together at a time, and then only when the need was present. I was eager to get to my stand, and had high hopes for the hunt. Suddenly I remembered something.

"Stop the truck," I said. "We've got to go back to the lodge. I forgot my release aid."

He stopped, turned around and began driving back to the lodge. I was frustrated, embarrassed, disappointed, ticked off, and sure I had ruined my best opportunity to tag a good buck. Eventually the guide got tired of my complaining and stopped the truck.

"Listen," he said, in a fatherly sort of way. "Never go into the woods worrying that you're getting there too late, or worrying that you have to come back too soon, or that you don't have enough time."

It would be a better story, I suppose, if I could say I tagged a big buck that day. I didn't. But the advice was valuable.

Still, saying it is one thing, doing it another. How is it done? One hunter I know has a routine. In effect, he has trained himself to disengage from the workaday world by following the same steps each time he goes afield. He leaves his vehicle, walks a hundred yards or so into the woods, sits down against a tree, and remains there with his eyes closed for five or ten minutes. He does this every time he hunts, no matter the time or place. When he resumes walking, he has left the world behind. He is relaxed but alert.

Deep breathing helps; don't laugh if you haven't tried it. Doctors, psychologists, shamans, and mystics have recommended it and practiced it for thousands of years. It's as simple as breathing very slowly and deeply for a minute or two. Try it, it works.

I try to avoid carrying a watch with me when I hunt. It's not always possible. Sometimes we must coordinate schedules with hunting buddies, or we are fitting in a morning hunt before an afternoon obligation of some sort. When possible, though, I leave the watch behind and do my best not to think about the time. If I must take a watch, I set the alarm for whenever I need to head back. It is unlikely the tiny beep of my watch will be heard for any distance, but I would set it anyway. The freedom to forget about time, even for a few hours, is more important to my enjoyment and my hunting success than the possibility that the alarm going off might spook game that has come onto the scene just as I am about to leave.

Shedding worries, relaxing, and forgetting about time is half the battle. Modern lifestyles affect the way we see and hear, too. In my book on turkey hunting, I recounted the story of the time I took a friend and neophyte hunter on a turkey hunt. At one point we flushed a turkey off a roost right over our heads, and he did not see or hear it. By that time, he was only confirming what I already knew: he wasn't going to see a turkey unless it was in the open and close, he wasn't going to hear a turkey unless it gobbled in his ear, and neither of those things was going to happen because he fidgeted and made so much

Author Rick Combs with nice buck he shot while in the zen zone!

noise that no turkey was ever going to get near him.

His case was an extreme example of habits that I think most modern people suffer from to varying degrees: the habit of seeing only what is directly in front of us, close up, and in the open, and tuning out most of the sounds around us.

When I was a youngster, my father, whose aging eyes were beginning to fail, regularly impressed me with his ability to spot game long before I could see it.

"Don't you see it?" he would whisper patiently as I strained my eyes for the deer or whatever he was pointing out.

"Look just to the left of that shagbark hickory, back in the shadows."

Still I couldn't see it. Eventually an ear would twitch or a tail would wag and I would spot it.

We rabbit hunted with beagles a lot in those days. Most of the rabbits we saw were naturally those we kicked up, or that the dogs jumped or began trailing. On nearly every outing, though, my father would manage to spot a rabbit or two sitting in its form. After a couple of years of practice I discovered that by concentrating, staying alert, and looking in the right places, I could spot them too. I also discovered over the years that if I didn't practice the skill, I could lose it.

I never forgot the lessons I learned from those experiences. Seeing game is not just a matter of visual acuity; it's a matter of knowing where to look, and what to look for.

I'm trying to teach my kids the skill. They want to look for a "deer." The trick, of course, is to look for part of a deer. Look for the horizontal line of the back crossing the vertical lines of the trees. Look for an ear, or the white of the throat or the belly. If the deer moves, it's easy to spot–assuming you are looking. Looking is harder than you think, and few of us can do it all the time.

Ever suddenly notice a deer right in front of your stand and wonder how it got there? It happens to me. There is only one way it got there without being spotted. You weren't looking. Yes, your eyes were open. That's not the same as looking. Chances are, your mind was elsewhere. Or maybe it was nowhere. The eyes don't see, the brain does.

Most of us are accustomed to tuning out irrelevant noise, and we do the same thing in the woods. The problem with that is that there is no irrelevant noise in the woods, unless we happen to be within hearing range of vehicles on the road, planes flying over, farm animals bellowing, or some of the other routine sounds of domestic life. Natural sounds in the woods are all conveying useful information of some sort, if we are only aware of it. The alert hunter hears the sounds of acorns falling from a white oak, the chuckling of a raccoon, the scraping sounds of a squirrel cutting a hickory nut. He hears the clatter of rocks when something crosses a nearby stream, the alarm putt of a hen turkey when it spots a coyote, the angry squawk of a jay when a hawk circles overhead, and the unmistakable sound of a fawn bleating for its mother. All these sounds and more convey information to the hunter about what might be going on where in the woods. When the woods grow suddenly quiet, the alert hunter becomes even more so.

Behavioral scientists talk about the "alpha state," a condition that can be measured by observing the electrical activity in the brain of individuals wired to a monitor. This particular electrical activity reveals itself in certain regular brain waves, and these waves invariably accompany a state of relaxed alertness and heightened creativity. We'll never know until a scientist begins monitoring the brain activity of hunters in the woods, but it could be that an "alpha state" is what the best hunters achieve in the woods.

How to get there? One way is through comfort. I'm all for discipline, but I suspect its over-rated. If you can remain alert, fully aware of your surroundings, and hunting effectively when you're cold and shivering, your back aches, or your feet hurt, more power to you. I recommend the opposite, though. Find out what it takes to make you as comfortable as you can be in the woods, and do what it takes to achieve it, whether that means wearing the right clothes, sitting in the right stand, using the right blind, or looking through the right sunglasses.

You'll know when you get there. Every sense is alive. You feel that you see everything and hear everything that goes on around you. You are relaxed but alert. You are confident. You have forgotten about time, and you are in no hurry, content to be exactly where you are, doing exactly what you are doing. There is a buck out there with your name on it. He is headed your way. ■

Other Outdoorsman's Edge Books Available From

WOODS N' WATER
PRESS

♦ **Successful Gun Trading**
   by George Knight

♦ **Deer Rifles & Cartridges**
   by Wayne vanZwoll, Ph.D.

♦ **Blood Trails II**
   by Ted Nugent

♦ **Hunting Rutting Bucks**
   by John Trout, Jr.

♦ **Wildlife & Woodlot Management Handbook**
   by Monte Burch

♦ **Muzzleloader Hunting: Then and Now**
   by Toby Bridges

♦ **Mounting Your Deer Head at Home**
   by Monte Burch

♦ **Sure-Fire Whitetail Tactics**
   by John Weiss

♦ **The Ultimate Guide to Planting Food Plots for Deer and Other Wildlife**
   by John Weiss

♦ **Finding Wounded Deer**
   by John Trout, Jr.

- **Butchering Deer:**
  The Complete Manual of Field Dressing,
  Skinning, Aging, and Butchering Deer at Home
  by John Weiss

- **Complete Guide to Rabbit Hunting: Secrets**
  of a Master Cottontail Hunter
  by David Fisher

- **The Art of Whitetail Deception: Calling,**
  Rattling and Decoying
  by Kathy Etling

- **Predator Hunting: Proven Strategies that**
  Work from East to West
  by Ron Spomer

- **Hunting Bears: Black, Brown, Grizzly, and Polar**
  Bears
  by Kathy Etling

- **Do-It-Yourself Gun Repair: Gunsmithing at Home**
  by Ed Matunas

- **Hunting Big Woods Bucks:**
  Secrets of Tracking and Stalking Whitetails
  by Master Guide Hal Blood

- **Antler, Bone, Horn and Hide:**
  Projects You Can Make at Home
  by Monte Burch

- **Advanced Turkey Hunting**
  by Richard Combs

TO ORDER,

Call us at 1-800-652-7527, write to us at Woods N' Water Press,
P.O. Box 550, Florida, NY 10921 or visit us on the web at
www.woodsnwaterpress.com or www.outdoorsmansedge.com.